STUDENT SUCCESS

*How to Succeed in College
and Still Have Time
for Your Friends*

STUDENT SUCCESS

*How to Succeed in College
and Still Have Time
for Your Friends*

Sixth Edition

Timothy L. Walter

University of Tulsa

Al Siebert

Portland State University

Harcourt Brace College Publishers

Fort Worth Philadelphia San Diego New York Orlando Austin San Antonio
Toronto Montreal London Sydney Tokyo

PUBLISHER: Ted Buchholz
ACQUISITIONS EDITOR: Eve Howard
PROJECT EDITOR: Barbara Moreland
PRODUCTION MANAGER: Mandy Manzano
BOOK DESIGNER: Bill Brammer
ELECTRONIC PUBLISHING SUPERVISOR: Michael Beaupré
ELECTRONIC PUBLISHING COORDINATORS: Barbara McGinnis
Kim Standish

Cover photography by Mark Humphries

Preface

Student Success is written for students who want to get the best education possible, earn good grades, and fully enjoy college life. Many students don't achieve these goals because they lack effective study strategies and have difficulty adjusting to the demands of college. You and every student can be successful, however, by choosing to use strategies for student success.

Learning how to learn takes effort at first. We know, because both of us struggled during our first years as college students. As psychology majors we gradually learned how to learn and to be successful. Later, as psychology instructors, we went out of our way to provide our students with practical information on how to learn faster, learn better, and cope well with all aspects of college life.

Student Success is the book we wish we had had when we started college. In writing it, our objectives have been to

1. give each student who uses it a better chance of graduating with a good education than students who do not use it.

2. provide specific, practical study skills that show how to gain quickly an understanding of the material in each course and get good grades.

3. enhance self-development. *Student Success* must help each student take control of his or her lifelong self-education and personal development.

Student Success is now in sixth edition because students who use the book report they receive better grades, learn more in less time, and have more time to enjoy college. As you read *Student Success*, you will discover the best way to make your college years truly valuable is to learn to study smarter, not harder. When you develop efficient and effective study skills, you do not have to choose between being a secluded, bleary-eyed bookworm and a less academically successful but socially fulfilled student. Student Success shows you how to be a successful student and still have time to do things with friends, play sports, take naps, socialize, date, watch television, keep up your fitness, go to concerts, and do what is personally important to you.

Student Success is also written for working students because more and more students are working while attending college. Working students don't have time to waste. Working students need efficient and effective strategies that help them achieve a good education and still have time to devote to work and outside interests.

This sixth edition of *Student Success* includes many new features and strategies to enhance your success. We have included feedback from students and instructors at the hundreds of colleges using this book in their "student success" programs.

New to this edition are expanded discussions of the following topics:

Strategies for critical thinking

Coping with stress and the frustrations associated with college

Managing your time

Learning to live in a diverse society

Coping with depression, loneliness, and shyness

Using university resources

Succeeding as a working student

Understanding and managing angry and negative feelings that can ruin friendships and hinder your learning

Student Success is more interactive than ever. Each chapter begins with a Self-Assessment to help you focus on what you can learn from the chapter. As you read you will find more self-assessment opportunities for answering questions about yourself and how you manage life as a student. Your answers to the questions will help you see what you are now doing to be a successful student and what changes you might wish to make. The self-assessments are our way of emphasizing that *your success in college comes more from making choices than from following instructions.* It is up to you to decide which strategies will be best for you.

Take a quick look through the book to get a feeling for what it covers. As you do, you might ask yourself questions such as:

What must I do to be successful in college?

How can studying be easier?

What strategies can I use to improve my understanding of what I read?

What are the tips on how to do well on exams?

How can I write better papers more rapidly?

Why is there an entire unit on time management?

How can I deal with anger and negative feelings?

How can I think more critically and productively?

How can I enjoy classes taught by all instructors, even those I find less interesting?

How do I deal with the typical problems that make students unhappy?

How can I learn to understand, appreciate, and get along with people who are very different from me?

How can I have more good friends?

What does it mean to view life as a school?

Student Success contains the answers to these and many more questions that students ask. *Student Success* is "user friendly." It shows you how things work. It provides you with a practical, flexible program for success in college that you can adapt and modify to fit your needs. When you use *Student Success* you are in control of your education!

We hope you have many successes during your college years!

Tim Walter and Al Siebert

Contents

STUDENT SUCCESS

*How to Succeed in College
and Still Have Time
for Your Friends*

part one

How to Succeed in College

❏   *Getting an Education: Not Easy but Worth It*

❏   *Your College Resources*

❏   *Your Inner Resources: Learning the Difference Between More Successful and Less Successful Students*

1

Getting an Education: Not Easy but Worth It

Imagine that you are one of a small group of students chosen to go on a tour of the new Starship Enterprise while it is in port for maintenance and equipment upgrades. Your tour guide, Ensign Evard, greets you when your shuttlecraft lands. She takes you through engineering where you see Geordi LaForge supervising systems tests. You visit the holodeck, the living quarters, and the transporter room. In the sick bay you see Dr. Crusher learning how to operate some new medical equipment.

You have lunch in Forward Seven with a science officer. The food synthesizer produces the meal you ask for in less than ten seconds. "If we had a food service like this," one of your companions says, staring at his steaming burrito with rice and beans, "no one would have anything to complain about!"

Your last stop is the Bridge, where Commander Data is busy at one of the consoles. A junior officer leads your group to each station and explains the controls.

As you gather around the captain's chair Ensign Evard instructs the computer to play a selection of video segments from the logs of the Enterprise. In the final scene Mr. Spock appears on the forward screen in his long robes. He raises his hand, palm open. He makes a four fingered "V" and says "May you live long and prosper."

You stand transfixed, deep in thought. You are startled when Commander Data, standing nearby, asks "Is something bothering you?"

"No," you say, "I was just wondering if I will live long and prosper in today's world."

"The probability," Data says, "is strong that you will."

"How do you know?"

"Because you are a college student," Data says. "Studies of human longevity and average lifetime income show that both have a strong positive correlation with education level."

"Really?" you ask.

"The studies in this matter are conclusive," he says. "For your species a college degree is predictive of both a longer life span and a lifetime income significantly greater than that of adults without a higher education. If you persist in your college studies you will increase the probability that, as Mr. Spock said, you will live long and prosper."

SURVIVING IN A NEW ENVIRONMENT

Did you know that 40 percent of the students in your freshman class will not be with the class when it graduates four years from now? About 20 percent will drop out and never graduate. The other 20 percent will "stop out" for a while but will return to finish their programs and graduate later. Some colleges have better percentages and some have worse, but nationwide that is how the statistics average out.

Why do so many students drop out or stop out? Why is college a struggle for many of the students who stay with it all the way? One of the main reasons is that many students can't handle the change from a *teaching* environment to a *learning* environment.

Until now, during all your years in grade school and high school, you have been in a *teaching* environment. How much you learned was strongly determined by the skills of your teachers. They had to have years of training to become certified. They had to continue taking courses to remain certified. They were evaluated by how well you and your classmates did on various tests.

College is a *learning* environment. The responsibility for what you learn is yours, not the instructor's. If all the students in a class do poorly on a test, the instructor is not held accountable. You will discover—perhaps to your amazement—that some college instructors do not have to have any formal training on how to teach college classes. They have not taken any courses in how to teach effectively. In some cases, to be hired as instructors they have only to be qualified as knowledgeable in their field. Most instructors with excellent teaching skills have become that way through personal, self-motivated efforts.

As Larry Smith, co-author of the *Instructor's Manual* for *Student Success* says, "The name of the game is *learning*, not *teaching*!" You are responsible for how well you handle your new environment. No one else is responsible. No one will accept the blame if you don't do well.

At the same time, however, you have not been abandoned. There are many resources and helpful people available to assist you in your effort to do well in college. In *Student Success* you will find much useful information about what you can do. Here is an example.

WHAT GRADUATING SENIORS SAY

Graduating seniors from nine colleges were asked what factors contributed significantly to or detracted from a successful and satisfying college career.

Based on replies from 2,379 students, the factors shown in the table below were identified.

Percentage of Students Who Said the Factor Contributed to a Successful and Satisfying College Career

Factor	Percentage
Personal contacts with students	89
Personal contacts with faculty and staff	78
Time I have spent on special interests and activities out of class	76
Ability to organize tasks and use my time effectively	73
Work experience during college or in the summer	72
Health, attitude, eating and drinking habits, other personal factors	63
Social life on campus	62
Sense of direction; knowing why I am in college and what career I would like to work toward	56
Availability of financial resources	52

As you can see from this study, it is important to make time with your friends a high priority. It is important to have friendly contacts with faculty and staff, to be involved in outside interests and to organize your time well, even to work while in school.

HOW *STUDENT SUCCESS* WILL BE USEFUL TO YOU

If your self-ratings reflect a difference between where you are now and what you want to be able to do in the future, *Student Success* will be very helpful. In

S E L F   A S S E S S M E N T

What Do You Think It Takes?

Do you have the "right stuff"? Have you thought about what it takes to succeed in college? Have you assessed your strengths and weaknesses?

Look at the following list of factors that have been found to affect success in college. Give yourself a score in each item—1 is weak, not something you do well; 2 means you can sometimes; 3 is in the middle, you can do reasonably well when you try; 4 means you are pretty good at it but could be better; 5 is strong or well-developed, a reliable strength.

Rate yourself twice. First indicate where you are now, second where you would like to be in the future.

I am able to:

now   future

___ ___   1. Start conversations with students I don't know and develop new friendships.

___ ___   2. Maintain good communications with my family members.

___ ___   3. Organize my time well and follow a flexible schedule that gives me time for studying, friends, and other activities.

___ ___   4. Study for a planned amount of time every day and then stop.

___ ___   5. Read textbooks rapidly.

___ ___   6. Comprehend and understand what I read.

___ ___   7. Take lecture notes and reading notes that I find useful as I prepare for exams.

___ ___   8. Feel confident about the way I prepare for exams.

___ ___   9. Feel calm while taking exams.

___ ___ 10. Do well on all kinds of examinations.

___ ___ 11. Do good library research and write excellent papers.

___ ___ 12. Motivate myself to reach goals I set for myself.

___ ___ 13. Accept complete responsibility for being successful without blaming instructors, roommates, family, or friends for my lack of success.

___ ___ 14. Appreciate myself for my accomplishments and good qualities. I like myself and how I live my life.

___ ___ 15. Locate and use resources available to me. I actively search for resources rather than passively waiting for others to tell me what to do.

___ ___ 16. Enjoy spending time with other students talking about what we are doing to get the most out of college.

___ ___ 17. Handle times when I feel awkward, shy, embarrassed, depressed, lonely, rejected, and a failure.

___ ___ 18. Hold up under stress and pressure.

___ ___ 19. Recognize signs of addiction to alcohol and other drugs.

___ ___ 20. Protect myself against realistic dangers.

___ ___ 21. Take action to resolve conflicts with instructors.

___ ___ 22. Enjoy being playful, curious, and humorous.

___ ___ 23. Feel comfortable with many opposite personality qualities such as being both calm and emotional, introverted and extroverted, smart and naive, and so on.

___ ___ 24. Learn useful lessons from unpleasant experiences without feeling like a victim.

Student Success you will find valuable information about why students fail in college and why students succeed. Every chapter covers aspects of being a student that, if not handled well, reduce your chances of graduating and that, if handled well, improve your chances of graduating. It's that simple.

Part One covers resources available to you and shows you how to use them. Here in Chapter 1 you are learning how to use *Student Success* as a resource. At the end of the chapter you will find suggestions on ways to form friendship groups right now, when you need them most.

Chapter 2 shows how to use your college catalog, orient yourself quickly, and locate the many free resources available to you.

Chapter 3 describes how to get maximum value from your most important resource of all, *you!* In Chapter 3 you will learn about important inner factors that influence success in college. (Note: It isn't I.Q.!)

Part Two focuses on how to manage your time and how to study efficiently. In Chapter 4 you will learn how to manage a tight schedule even when you work and have other important activities.

Psychologists have spent nearly 100 years studying human learning. Chapters 5 and 6 provide you with the most practical information available on learning how to learn. Chapter 5 shows how to set and achieve study goals. Chapter 6 shows how to organize your efforts so that you can learn more with less time and effort.

Part Three gives you an effective plan for passing your college courses with high grades. Chapter 7 covers a study method called "SQ4R." It is the most effective, well-proven study method available. Chapter 8 focuses on how to pass tests with high grades. This chapter includes examples of all kinds of tests—multiple choice, true-false, essay, short answer, and so forth. Chapter 9 offers you practical tips on how to use your library well and write "A" papers.

Part Four covers how to handle the human side of college life. Poor relationships with instructors, friends, and family can be emotionally draining.

Chapter 10 shows you how to overcome false expectations and erroneous beliefs about instructors. It helps you handle disillusionments about instructors in a way that is healthy.

If you want to improve the instruction you get, what can you do? Chapter 11 shows how to influence your instructors to get positive results.

Concerns about being liked and accepted by friends and family often distract college students from their studies and make them vulnerable to peer pressures. Chapter 12 shows how to develop good friendships. This chapter also covers how to gain support from your family.

Part Five digs into some of the most difficult aspects of college life today. Chapter 13 takes a realistic look at serious hazards and dangers you face as a college student.

In Chapter 14 we focus on two emotional states that, when not handled well, can undercut all your efforts to succeed in college. They are anger and negativity.

The many stresses of college life will either strengthen or weaken you. People who are life's best survivors find ways to cope with difficulties and gain strength from adversity. Chapter 15 describes how to develop a survivor personality. It shows you how to learn useful lessons in the school of life.

Tim Walter has extensive experience helping student athletes succeed academically. Student athletes will find good academic coaching in a special appendix.

Guidelines for Action

Success comes not from what you read or hear but from what you do with what you learn. At the end of each chapter you will find an Action Checklist or a set of Action Guidelines. These show how to apply the information and strategies in the chapter. They show how to use the material in the chapter and acquire the methods as useful skills.

Friendship Groups Increase Successes in College

You can facilitate your learning and deepen your enjoyment of college life by talking frequently with a group of friendly classmates about your experiences, questions, feelings, and observations. At the end of each chapter you will find suggestions for questions and issues to discuss or activities to undertake with supportive friends. (Note: If being friends with people is a bit difficult for you, read Chapter 12 right away. Skip around in the book whenever you wish.)

Many colleges and universities offer a course to help beginning students succeed. In it you will meet regularly with a group of other first year students to talk about the challenges of college. These courses are often offered for credit. Check your college catalog to see if some kind of "College Success Seminar" is offered. It will be worth taking. Research conducted at the University of South Carolina, for example, shows that students enrolled in a course called "University 101" have a significantly better survival rate in college (Fidler, 1991).

It is a good idea to pair up with one or two other students for the purpose of being successful in college—a version of the "buddy system." It is different from having a good roommate or a good friend on campus. The idea of college success partners is to interact with each other for the purpose of facilitating each other's success in college. Frequent interactions with one or two other students who agree to use *Student Success* will help you increase your successes in college.

THE BIG PICTURE

Student Success is a practical, "user friendly" book. It covers all aspects of the psychology of succeeding in college. The key to its value, however, is you. *Student Success* is not a formula, recipe, or blueprint for success. The book is written for individuals who feel responsible for how well their lives work out. In every challenging situation we talk about how your reaction and your way of interacting with it determines the outcome.

Student Success is for self-motivated individuals who need to do things their own way. It is for students who reject being programmed about what to think, feel, and do. How can it be otherwise? Surviving in an environment that is not always safe requires alertness and your own unique solutions to unexpected situations.

You are living in a world much different from the one in which your parents and teachers grew up. To survive and thrive in a rapidly changing world you must learn how to orient yourself quickly to new circumstances and manage change well.

You will probably have three or four careers and live an active, healthy life of up to 100 years old. National boundaries are blurring. The planet is becoming an integrated community. To succeed in your careers, business activities, or profession you must be able to adapt to different cultures, different values, different beliefs, and different life-styles.

Critical thinking skills will be essential for handling rapid changes in the world—changing values, conflicting perspectives, and unexpected developments that carry both opportunities and dangers. Thus, your time in college is a major transition. By learning how to handle challenges well, you will emerge prepared for whatever you encounter. You will have self-confidence. You will be a resilient person with good judgment and reliable inner strengths.

Whether you get stronger in college or become overwhelmed by it is up to you. *Student Success* can show you how to survive your freshman year, improve your chances of succeeding in your courses, enjoy your college years, get a good education, and graduate with your class.

College is more than an opportunity to learn, however. It is also an important way to grow, mature, and develop as a person. *Student Success* provides you with guidelines on how to manage your personal growth and development, and how to convert stresses, strains, and rough times into strengthening experiences.

SUCCESS GROUP ACTIVITIES

To get started meet where you can talk with some privacy. Take turns asking each other about your first reactions, feelings, and impressions of college. An important ingredient for a good session is to make sure that each person feels he or she has been heard.

By the end of the session make sure that each person has the feeling, "Other people know what I am feeling and experiencing here." To accomplish this aim, someone may have to interrupt a long-winded talker who doesn't know how to stop. Someone may have to ask encouraging questions of the person who is rather quiet and not used to being listened to by a group. These are matters that your group will have to learn to handle, if they come up.

A more structured group activity will be to spend some time talking with each other about the question, "Do you intend to graduate with our class?" Other related questions are, "Why are you here in college? Why this college rather than another? Was going to college your idea? Your parents? Whose idea was it?" And "Have you selected a major yet? Do you have specific career goals?"

Another useful focus for your group is to write a list comparing the differences between being a high school student and being a college student. Some freshmen don't survive because they expect college to be a sort of postgraduate high school. It isn't. The two worlds are so different that many students cannot handle the "transition shock." As you will see, we have written an entire chapter focusing on the problems many students have in dealing with their frustrations and anger about their college experience.

So talk with each other about what you expected from college and what you have found. Just getting it down on paper (or on a computer screen) helps you get a handle on the situation. Then as the days and weeks go by you can revise and update your list as necessary.

Plan on taking several hours to go through these activities. If a long session isn't possible, hold several shorter ones.

During your first two weeks on campus it will be helpful to meet frequently. Then meet less often as you settle in. But frequency of meetings is up to you. The activity of meeting with supportive friends is more important than the schedule.

REQUEST: We would like to know how these and other suggestions in *Student Success* work for you. Please write to us at the address in the back of the book and let us know. Also tell us what you come up with on your own. Thanks.

2

Your College Resources

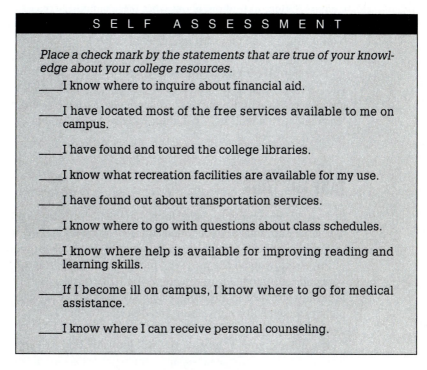

S E L F   A S S E S S M E N T

Place a check mark by the statements that are true of your knowledge about your college resources.

____I know where to inquire about financial aid.

____I have located most of the free services available to me on campus.

____I have found and toured the college libraries.

____I know what recreation facilities are available for my use.

____I have found out about transportation services.

____I know where to go with questions about class schedules.

____I know where help is available for improving reading and learning skills.

____If I become ill on campus, I know where to go for medical assistance.

____I know where I can receive personal counseling.

BE ASSERTIVE ABOUT ORIENTATION

Even though the orientation leaders try to inform you of every facility and service available to you, they are bound to overlook something. This chapter describes the college support services and facilities you should know about. You can use this chapter as your checklist. As you go through orientation, become familiar with all the services and facilities we list that are offered by your college.

If you have completed an orientation program, use this chapter to review your knowledge of campus services. Orientation is a continuous process throughout your college career. You will need the use of various resources. Make sure you know what they offer and where they are located.

If during your orientation it appears to you that a service or facility isn't going to be mentioned, ask about it. If you still don't find out all you want to know, make sure you search out more information on your own. Make an active effort to get information quickly about your college, campus, and surrounding area. Be assertive. Don't stay away from a support service because of rumors or negative advice.

If possible, pay a visit to every service or facility to check it out. For example, most colleges have Learning Skills Centers and Writing Improvement Centers. Often, to find out about what these support services can offer you, you'll need to stop in and have a chat with a staff member. Don't hesitate. You'll usually find that staff members of college support services are trying to think up ways to insure that students make use of their services.

Take a stroll over to the Intramural Sports Center, the Office of Financial Aid, or to any one of the libraries on campus. You may pick up a few ideas about ways in which you want to spend your time on campus. You may learn about financial help you didn't know was available to students like yourself.

TAKE THE TOUR

Most colleges provide guided tours during your orientation program. By all means, take advantage of your orientation tour wherever and whenever it occurs.

During your orientation program, you'll probably be provided with loads of information about the program, facilities, and opportunities available at your college. Among the information, you'll often find a "survival kit," which is usually provided by the college admissions office. Your packet should explain procedures for registration and describe various services and facilities available to you.

If you look around campus, you will probably find free copies of the college newspaper. College newspapers often put out a special "orientation edition" to acquaint new students with various activities on campus.

The checklist of college services and activities we've provided is typical of what you would often find at a larger school. Whether your college has more or fewer of the places we've listed, use our list as a starting point as you acquaint yourself with your campus.

The more quickly you become familiar with your campus, the more you will feel at home. Learn why certain offices and facilities exist, even if you don't use them now. At some point it may be to your advantage to know where and why most offices and services exist.

COLLEGE ORIENTATION CHECKLIST

Academic Advising

Your college has advisors available to tell you about course requirements for different programs, when classes are scheduled, what sequences of courses to take, and how to get the courses you want. Even if you have looked through the catalog and know what courses you want, you will probably have to obtain an advisor's approval to enroll in the courses.

Academic Affairs

Most likely you will have to go at some time to the academic affairs office for assistance with questions or problems having to do with changing a mistake in your transcript of grades, removing an "incomplete" in a course, getting permission to take more than the allowed number of course hours, waiving a course requirement, getting into a course already filled, or arranging for special academic programs.

Activity Center or Student Union

In the center where students hang out, you will find cafeterias, art displays, television rooms, reading rooms, possibly even a bowling alley, barber shop, Ping-Pong tables, or pool tables. The student union on every campus is unique, so take time to walk around and familiarize yourself with this building. On the bulletin boards you will find announcements for theater offerings and for the college film offerings. Student groups frequently organize film festivals which show films not available in the regular theaters in your community.

Admissions, Orientation Director, Office for Reentry Students

The people who work in admissions or orientation offices were hired to help the person who has questions and needs information about starting classes. On larger campuses these will probably be separate offices. On smaller campuses they will be combined. In any case, go to them first.

Adult Center

Most schools now have at least a room, sometimes called the Senior's Center, where the older student can go to get information about any problems, concerns, or questions that may come up.

Bookstore

Take some time to go through the bookstore. Browse around to see where different books are located. Usually the front part of the store contains what is called "trade" books. These are books available to the general public and available in almost all bookstores. At the back of the store you will probably find the textbook section. The books will be arranged on shelves listed by course numbers within the different departments of the college. The bookstore will probably have ordered and stocked for courses that you will be taking. Instructors must place their orders several months before classes start so textbooks are available when you arrive.

After registering for your courses, it is wise to purchase your textbooks right away. If you wait until the first class meeting to hear the instructor tell you what to buy, the bookstore might be sold out. Also, if the instructor is using the same textbook again this year, you may find used copies of the book available. Be careful to purchase only the most recent edition of a textbook, however. Using the third edition of a textbook when the instructor has now switched to the fourth edition will not be acceptable.

Campus Security

Find out how to get help from campus security in case of an emergency. They are the people to call first when any sort of help from police is needed. Make friends with the security officers. They appreciate it.

Career Counseling

College students today, more than ever before, are entering with a focus on career opportunities. The career center counselors have a wealth of information and assessment instruments to help students explore career possibilities. In today's fast changing world new career options emerge every few months. The career center will probably have computer programs set up, so you can spend a few minutes at a terminal answering questions and then receive a print-out about what to consider exploring.

Cashier's Office

All monetary matters involving tuition are handled by the cashier. The cashier's office may cash checks for any person with a valid student body identification card.

Counseling Center

The counseling center is staffed with professional counselors available for private sessions with students who need to talk about personal matters, including concerns about AIDS, pregnancy, relationships, problems from being abused as a child, or being the adult child of an alcoholic parent. When certain problems become too difficult than a person can cope with, the psychologists and counselors who work in these centers are especially trained to help.

Day-Care Center

For students with preschool children, the college may provide day-care. Parents can bring a child to school and, for a low fee, have the child cared for by specialists.

Dean of Students

The dean of students is responsible for seeing that you are well taken care of in school and that any problems you have can be solved. It is likely that if you go to the dean of students' office you will be referred to another office. That's okay. Their job is to know where to send you and how to find the answers that you need.

Employment Office

A separate office usually exists to coordinate job offers from local employers with students who are looking for off-campus work. There are many jobs in every community that fit perfectly with being a student. These range from part-time sales work, where you work at hours of your own choosing, to some sort of night work, where you mainly have to sit and watch equipment running.

Financial Aid Office

Scholarships are only one form of aid or financial support offered to students. There are organizations which provide grants to needy students. A grant is an outright gift, which does not have to be repaid. In some instances, for a person who is without funds, the college may have a way to reduce tuition fees. Most students qualify for loans at very low interest rates. These funds are provided by the federal government, and by other sources.

If you are a veteran, you probably know about your GI benefits provided by the federal government; but do you also know that schooling benefits may be provided by your state? The office of financial aid can tell you if you qualify.

Another source of funds is through student employment, or "work-study programs." There are many jobs available on-campus for students who need income. These jobs don't pay a great deal, but they are on-campus and are usually flexible to fit with the student's class schedule.

Business majors and many others have a great opportunity with the cooperative education program. You get college credit while being paid to work in selected, approved jobs. This is a cooperative program co-sponsored by employers and colleges. Many students go on to be hired by their co-op employers after graduation.

Handicapped Student Services

Special assistance is available to handicapped students. This assistance may include readers for visually impaired students, or signers for the hearing impaired. The assistance counselors have many practical suggestions, including information about how to obtain special equipment and learning aids.

Health Service

Every campus has a medical unit of some kind available for emergency medical care and treatment. It is useful to know where this center is and what services are provided before you need help from them.

The health service on your campus is probably a resource for information, programs, and services on human sexuality, birth control, prevention of venereal disease, and so on. The health service may also have people trained to deal with alcohol and drug abuse problems.

Learning Center

Many schools have established special centers where you go in order to learn a specific subject. You check in and tell the person in charge what you want. You will then likely be assigned to a booth with a set of earphones, a television monitor, or a computer terminal. You work at your own speed at the lesson and can stay with it as long as you wish. The person in charge will be glad to explain to you how everything works.

Legal Services Office

Larger colleges have legal information and counseling available to students. They can provide information about your state's auto insurance requirements, handling involvement in automobile accidents or drunk driving tickets, landlord and tenant agreements, state and federal wage laws, employment discrimination matters, consumer protection, small claims court actions, and family law.

Library

Visit the library and take some time to walk through it. You will find that all the stacks are open. You can go almost any place in the library and see what is available. You will notice that in the library there are many desks and study areas available. You might consider picking a spot in the library for your regular place to study.

Librarians usually enjoy telling people about all the library services. Take advantage of this good will. Plan to learn, as soon as possible, about how to use the microfilm equipment. It is not as complicated as it may look to you. Many library materials are stored on microfilm, so it is important to learn what to do if you need to use the equipment.

Find out if there is more than one library on campus. You may discover that there is a "reserve" library where instructors place materials on reserve for classes to prevent certain books from being checked out. Some departments at the college have their own libraries, and there may be a library for graduate students.

Museums and Archives

Many colleges and universities have received museums and archives from private donors. These collections may be housed in their own buildings somewhere near campus. Find out about these unusual opportunities. The staff will appreciate your interest and you may get much more of an education by exploring these places than you expect.

Outdoor Recreation

Want to go on a rafting trip on the weekend? Cross country skiing? Sailing or canoeing? Hiking? Many colleges have special programs available. You can check out equipment for outdoor activities or sign up for an outdoor activity led by someone specially trained for the job.

Registrar

The registrar's office is responsible for keeping all academic records. This is the office you go to if you are confused about a grade that you have received or which may have been recorded incorrectly. If you have taken classes elsewhere, at anytime in the past, the registrar's office can give you information on how to claim credit and obtain documentation so that it will apply to your program. After you graduate, the registrar's office provides transcripts which may be requested in the future.

Sports Center

Be sure to check the sports facility. As a student, you have access at certain times to the gymnasium, swimming pool, racquet ball courts, and tennis courts. Take your time to inquire, because having a nice swim between classes some day might be exactly the right thing for you. There will be an exercise room which you can use when available and there may be a track for jogging, basketball courts, and other possibilities for exercise.

Student Housing

Your school may provide student housing in its own dormitories. It will also coordinate placement of students into private homes and facilities that exist in the nearby area. Many landlords will register the availability of housing with this office.

Study Skills Center

This center is staffed with specialists in teaching people how to read faster, remember better, pass tests more easily, and, in general, succeed in the academic aspects of school. Improving study skills often is the solution to dealing with "emotional problems."

Transportation Office

If you have to commute to school you may need a permit to park in the campus parking lots. Be sure to find out about car pools and university buses as an alternative to driving you own car each day.

Around Campus

As you travel around campus, you will encounter small groups of students encouraging you to join in their activities. You will find activity groups that are interested in having you become a jogger, hiker, bike rider, chess player, or perhaps a player of "new age" games. You may be invited to join the school choir or band. There are many action groups on campus that will seek your support.

Be prepared to have students ask you to sign petitions to support the development of solar energy, save whales, fight world hunger, stop the development of nuclear power plants, protect the environment from oil spills, stop the dumping of toxic chemicals into the earth and water, free political prisoners, control the world's population explosion, control animal population through neuter and spay programs, or legalize marijuana. Whether you support any of these activities or not, the fact is, they are a part of campus life today.

REMEMBER: The entire school exists to assist you in succeeding in getting the education you want! Take time now, before you get into your academic program, to get acquainted with your school. You will feel more comfortable more quickly, become more fully absorbed in classes, and enjoy the excitement of learning and discovering new ideas without being confused about what's going on around you.

Important Places Near Campus

Walk along the streets near your campus and locate any of the following that may be important for you to know about:

____ post office

____ copy centers

____ 24-hour bank machines

____ laundromats, dry cleaners

____ bank branches

____ grocery stores

____ eating places, ice-cream shops

____ clothing stores

____ service stations

____ bike repair shop

____ churches

____ church-sponsored student centers

____ drugstores

____ bookstores

____ parks

❏ ACTION GUIDELINES: Around Campus

As an aid to getting oriented to your college, list the places on campus that you would like to know more about and write out several questions about each that you would like to have answered.

Name of center or service: _____

Questions: _____
_____
_____

Name of center or service: _____

Questions: _____
_____
_____

Name of center or service: _____

Questions: _____
_____
_____

SUCCESS GROUP ACTIVITY: Learning Team

Become a "learning team." Each of you could pick certain places to find out about. Go ask questions. Take notes. Get enough handouts for everyone. Then come back and give each other a report.

3

Your Inner Resources: Learning the Differences Between More Successful and Less Successful Students

S E L F   A S S E S S M E N T

Place a check mark by the statements that are true of you.

_____I know that the way I daydream influences my success in school and in life.

_____I can be both optimistic and pessimistic about reaching my goals.

_____I know I can influence the way my life goes.

_____My feelings of self-esteem and self-confidence are strong and healthy.

"MOST LIKELY TO SUCCEED"

David McClelland, a Harvard psychology professor, startled the business world in the 1960s. He developed a test that could accurately predict which college students would achieve the most career success 20 years later!

What was the key? A test of imagination. After years of carefully controlled scientific research conducted on thousands of people in many different countries,

McClelland proved that he could predict a person's future from the pattern of the person's daydreams.

A few years later McClelland stirred up even more interest in his work when he reported the results of a major research project with businessmen in India. He had selected India for his research because, of all English-speaking cultures, people in India are most extreme in believing that external events and their station in life control their lives. In India, McClelland proved that with a few days of instruction, Indian businessmen could learn to use their minds in the ways that high achievers do. Then during the two years that followed, the experimental group, who had learned how to think as high achievers do, significantly outperformed a carefully matched control group.

What does McClelland's research mean to you? Many things. First, your mind can be the best resource you have, if you learn to use it well. Second, daydreams serve as a blueprint for your future. Third, the mental habit pattern that makes a person more successful can be learned. Fourth, it doesn't take long to learn how to use your mind in ways that make you more successful.

Mental Activities that Lead to Success

McClelland's research demonstrated that if you practice thinking about being successful in certain ways, you are more likely to be successful.

Persons with the following pattern in their daydreams can be predicted to be more successful than others. In their daydreams the main character in the story:

1. is working to achieve a goal, do something better, or accomplish something challenging;

2. has a strong need and an emotional desire to reach the goal and anticipates the feelings of satisfaction and accomplishment that success will bring;

3. thinks through the details of how to succeed despite obstacles, difficulties, personal limitation, possible problems, or barriers; and matches own level of ability against the situation to determine that the challenge is neither too easy nor too difficult;

4. consults various resources for information about ways to handle obstacles and reach the goal but retains control over decision and responsibility for the outcome.

Successful people anticipate future actions with a mixture of hope and worry. After thinking in the manner described above, people who decide to "go for it" can make a total emotional commitment to succeed and realistically expect to succeed.

The four mental activities leading to accomplishment and achievement all occur before a motivated effort is made to reach the goal. Few people understand that the process a person goes through before selecting a goal has a significant effect on the chances of success.

In summary, for you to feel successful, your goal must be:

    self-chosen

    moderately challenging

    motivating

    slightly risky

    possible to reach with good effort.

SELF ASSESSMENT

Think about your decision to attend college. Check off the criteria for successful goal-setting present in your decision to attend college and pursue a degree.

____My decision to attend college was primarily my own; it was self-chosen.

____The goal of getting a college degree is at least moderately challenging, if not very challenging.

____The idea of being a college graduate makes me feel successful. I feel motivated to work hard and reach my goal.

____Attending college feels risky. I feel a little nervous, but it is a pleasant, exciting nervousness.

____I believe I *can* reach my goal of graduating from college if I make a solid effort.

____I believe I *will* reach my goal of earning a college degree.

In a visioning session with students in a freshman seminar, Gary went through the four elements of goal selection outlined by McClelland. He reconsidered aiming for a 4.0 grade point average (GPA) his first term. He sized up each of his courses, listed the difficulties he expected with them, and for each one set a realistic grade he felt he could earn. He took into account the resources available to him—*Student Success*, the learning center, his own abilities, and so on. He decided to aim for a 3.2 GPA.

For a goal to give you a feeling of achievement when it is reached, it must have a specific, observable, measurable result that you attain by a specified time. Saying "I want to get good grades" won't work! Selecting a target grade for each course or a certain GPA for each term has a specific, measurable end

Reprinted by permission of UFS, Inc.

result that is attainable in a designated time. Then when the date arrives you definitely know if you achieved your goal or not.

What Works: Practical Positive and Practical Negative Thinking

Successful students spend time anticipating difficulties they might encounter when trying to reach their goals. Is it being negative to worry about what could go wrong? No. Not in the sense of being a negative person.

Mental and emotional flexibility comes from being able to think and feel in both positive and negative ways about situations. A person who is always positive and seldom negative has as much difficulty coping well as a person who is always negative and seldom positive.

A practical person, one with a flexible outlook, combines practical positive thinking with practical negative thinking. Trying to do only one without the other is like trying to drive a car with no reverse gear.

SELF ASSESSMENT

Successful students are students who do well despite the negative factors they encounter. Place a mark before the ones you have anticipated or that you believe might happen to you.

___✓Being successful may take more energy.

___✓I may work harder than less-committed students.

___✓I will risk failure when aiming high.

___I will have less time for friends.

___I will have less time to loaf around.

___I may get eye strain, back strain, or neck strain.

___Sometimes, I will miss some fun because of studying for tests.

___People may expect more of me ("If I get a B, they may have a heart attack!").

___I may not be able to go out for sports as often because practice will interfere with studying.

___I may be razzed and called a "bookworm."

___✓My family may get upset because I don't have as much time for them.

___If my grades drop a little, people may give me a bad time.

___✓Some people may think I'm weird if I get top grades.

___I will have to learn too much too fast.

___It may be difficult to study hard and do well in a required course in which I am not interested.

Let's try it out for a moment. You probably have some positive expectations about the many benefits you would gain from doing well in college. But have you considered the case against doing well? Take a minute right now to answer this question: "If I choose to do really well in college, what are some of the problems and difficulties I might have to cope with?"

When you anticipate the problems and difficulties you may encounter on your way to a desired goal, you are better prepared emotionally to handle them when they occur. Psychologist Irving Janis showed in a research project that some worrying before going into something difficult helps you handle it better. People who don't worry at all and people who worry a great deal without practical problem solving don't handle difficulties as well. So keep in mind that a little worrying is useful when it takes place as one part of the entire pattern of problem solving.

Balancing the Consequences

Looking at some negative consequences of doing well decreases feelings of distress or discouragement *if* they occur. More importantly, however, successful students dream and think about the many payoffs for doing well.

Compare the negative statements you marked in the first self-assessment with the positive statements you marked in the second self-assessment. As you weigh the consequences—both negative and positive—of being a more successful student, you will feel more comfortable in establishing your educational goals. If you are like most students, you can see from assessing the advantages and disadvantages, your gains will far outweigh your losses.

S E L F   A S S E S S M E N T

Place a mark in front of all the positive things that can happen as a result of learning the habits used by successful students.

✓ I will become more efficient and effective at learning.

_____ What was hard work in the past will now feel much easier and come more naturally.

_____ I will have time for friends and not feel guilty.

_____ I will spend less time loafing and not feel that I am wasting my time and life.

_____ Some of the physical ailments, like eye and neck strain I once had may fade away with better study habits.

_____ The joy I receive from being more successful on tests will outweigh the feeling of missing out on other things I would do instead of studying.

✓ My self-esteem will improve.

_____ The perceptions of people important to me will improve.

_____ My family will be proud of me and understand that the time I do have to spend with them is important.

_____ I will become more interesting to myself as a result of all the new things that I learn

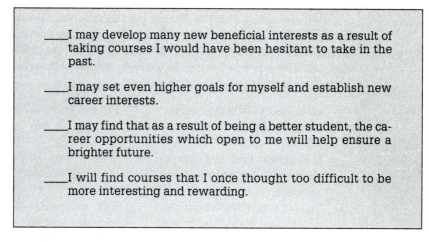

____I may develop many new beneficial interests as a result of taking courses I would have been hesitant to take in the past.

____I may set even higher goals for myself and establish new career interests.

____I may find that as a result of being a better student, the career opportunities which open to me will help ensure a brighter future.

____I will find courses that I once thought too difficult to be more interesting and rewarding.

INEFFECTIVE GOAL SETTING

Who Sets Your Goals?

The goal-setting done by many students is not self-motivated. The goal-setting occurs because of external pressures to have goals. By now you have become accustomed to having teachers, counselors, and advisors ask you to describe your career goals. That's fine, and the people asking you have good intentions. The achievement research, however, shows that how you identify, choose, and emotionally commit yourself to a goal is far more important than inventing one to tell people about.

What some students call goals are really wishes. They would like to have what they see others enjoying, but they don't know how to get it through personal effort. Such students frequently believe that external factors and luck determine how well things turn out.

Internally Rather Than Externally Motivated

One of the most difficult problems for most students entering college is having too much freedom. Throughout high school their lives were organized, controlled, and structured by external forces. When a test was scheduled, the teacher constantly reminded everyone and coached students on what they needed to know.

In college, an instructor might announce a test in five weeks and then never mention it again. To survive in college you have to keep yourself organized and self-directed.

Before continuing, check to find out your attitude about feeling in control of your life. Take several minutes to look at the following pairs of statements. Put a check mark by the statement in each pair that, in general, is closest to what you believe is true. Even if there is some truth to both statements, select the one that is more true than you think.

1. ✓ How hard I study determines the grades I get.
   ___ I would get better grades if the teaching in this school were better.

2. ___ It is useless to try to change another person's opinions or attitudes.
   ✓ When I want to, I can usually get others to see things my way.

3. ✓ The increasing divorce rate indicates that fewer people are trying to make their marriages last.
   ___ Fate determines how long a marriage will last. All you can do is hope your partner will stay with you for life.

4. ___ Finding a well-paying job is a matter of being luckier than the next guy.
   ✓ In our society a person's income is determined largely by ability.

5. ✓ Promotions are earned through hard work and persistence.
   ___ Promotions come from having the right people like you.

6. ✓ It is wishful thinking to believe that one can influence what happens in society at large.
   ___ People like me can change the course of world events by making ourselves heard.

7. ___ I am the master of my fate.
   ✓ When I see an unfortunate person, I sometimes think, "There but for the grace of God go I."

8. ___ Many people are difficult to get along with, so there is no use trying to be friendly.
   ✓ Getting along with people is a skill that can be learned.

9. ✓ I am usually a good influence on others.
   ___ Running around with bad company leads a person into bad ways.

10. ___ I would be much happier if people weren't so irritating.
    ✓ Peace of mind comes from learning how to adapt to life's stresses.

To score yourself, count all the check marks in the the left-hand column for the odd numbered items and the check marks in the right-hand column for all even-numbered items. Your score is the total number of checks in these places. (Note: you can count up to five check marks on each side but no more.)

The range of possible scores is zero to ten. Scores of eight or higher suggest you are more internally directed than students who get lower scores.

BEING IN CONTROL OF YOUR LIFE

The higher your score on this attitude survey, the more you feel that you have control over your life. Students who know they are personally responsible for many of the successes and failures that occur in their lives are called "high internals" by Julian Rotter and other social scientists. Such students believe that what controls the important forces and events in their lives is inside themselves.

Students with low scores often believe that they are the helpless pawns of fate. They tend to believe that forces influencing their lives are external to themselves. These students are called "high externals." The point we want to make here is that both sets of attitudes are correct. Each of these attitudes is self-validating. Students who are high internals believe they can influence much of what happens to them. They take actions to make things happen. The results of their efforts confirm their beliefs. Students who are high externals seldom take action. They believe it won't do any good. Then, sure enough, most of what happens to them is determined by outside forces and other people.

The fact that you are reading this book is an indication that you are probably a person who is "internal." You know that a book such as this can provide some practical tips on how to be more effective. People who are high "externals" respond to a book like this by saying, "It won't do me any good." These people are right. Their habitual way of responding to learning opportunities and chances for personal growth maintains their attitude that it doesn't do any good to try.

WHAT WORKS: COOPERATIVE NONCONFORMITY

College counselors see extreme differences in students. Some students are so determined to be self-reliant nonconformists they put energy into proving they can't be influenced by others. At the other extreme, some students passively wait to be told what to do. They drift from one person to another waiting for advice, guidance, and help. They accept directions from almost anyone, even when they don't need to be helped.

What works best is to balance self-reliance based on inner resources with an ability to accept guidance and direction from external resources. College life can be frustratingly difficult for the student who is always one way and seldom the other.

If you find this information about the relationship of personality factors to success in college useful, that's great! But you aren't done yet. There are more aspects of personality strongly related to being more successful or less successful in college. They are your "selfs."

HOW YOUR "SELFS" CONTROL YOUR SUCCESS

Your self-esteem, self-confidence, self-concept, and self-image control your successes in life. *Self-esteem* is your opinion of yourself. It is a feeling dimension. Without strong self-esteem your actions are controlled by worries about what others might think.

Unfortunately for many children, their parents program them never to brag, appear proud, or speak well of themselves. These parents have good intentions, of course. But the problem is that students with low self-esteem rarely do well in school. When students don't expect to do well, they don't. They can't handle success or praise so they avoid it.

Students with low self-esteem talk in ways their parents needed to hear. They typically put themselves down, constantly repeat how dumb or stupid they are, focus on their mistakes, and engage in a lot of self-criticism.

On the other side of the coin, there are students with inflated self-esteem. They constantly brag. They let everyone know how great they are. The problem is that people with inflated self-esteem can't engage in the kind of healthy self-criticism that leads to self-improvement.

Strong, healthy self-esteem is like a thick skin. It acts as a buffer to shrug off hurtful criticisms from others. It lets you appreciate compliments. It also determines how much you learn after something goes wrong.

Self-confidence controls your prediction of how well you will do in a new activity. It is an action dimension. People lacking self-confidence can't rely on themselves. People with strong self-confidence know that they can count on themselves more than anyone else. They expect to handle both adversit and opportunities successfully.

Self-concept is made up of your ideas about who and what you are. It is a thinking dimension. The nouns and adjectives you use to describe yourself during self-talk are like instructions. People with positive self-concepts and people with negative self-concepts all act in ways consistent with their beliefs about themselves.

Self-image determines what you, as a unique individual, strive to achieve, maintain, or avoid in your life circumstances. People with a poor self-image won't try to change or leave a bad situation at home or work. They may try to be successful by imitating successful people. Some try to cover up a weak self-image with impressive clothing, titles, high income, important friends, the right address, and other material "proofs" of success. They may try to build themselves up by tearing others down.

People with a strong self-image don't have to prove anything to anyone. They can wear any clothing, be friends with anyone, and live anywhere. They live a unique life that works for them. They have a positive, synergistic effect wherever they are. They encourage and applaud the successes of others.

A strong, positive self-image is the basis for becoming an excellent professional person. Such a person, guided by inner standards and values, is flexible, resilient, durable, and creatively effective. They find a way of working that is unique to them. Success is measured by excellent results and inner feelings of satisfaction. Prosperity, positions of power, honors, and outstanding success are not goals, but simply recognition for being responsible, effective, and needed. People without a strong, positive sense of their unique abilities are destined to be confined to jobs and roles created by other people.

It is important that you look at each one of these characteristics to determine what you are like and what you want to be. Building a strong "self" depends on how you want to think about yourself and how you want to behave, and it is totally under your control.

S E L F   A S S E S S M E N T

Which of the following is true of you?

____I am able to accept both praise and criticism.

____I can resist being manipulated by flattery and shrug off hostile comments.

____I don't engage in extreme self-criticism or self-praise.

____I usually feel I can count on myself.

____I am able to handle adversity as well as success.

____I usually think of myself in positive terms.

____When asked, I can describe my abilities and strengths to others.

____I can find something good in bad situations.

____I have learned how to manage my self-improvement.

____I don't try to cover up my weaknesses by trying to impress others.

____I don't try to build myself up by tearing others down.

____I encourage and applaud the successes of others.

____My feelings of success come from my work and my inner feeling of satisfaction.

____I believe I have unique qualities and skills.

HOW TO BUILD A STRONG TEAM OF "SELFS"

Increasing Self-Esteem

Self-esteem is the easiest to develop because it is the most verbal. It is strengthened by positive self-talk. If you have strong self-esteem it is fairly easy to make a list of all the things you like and appreciate about yourself.

Go ahead and make a list of the things that you like about yourself. Write out things that would be helpful to remind yourself of in good times and in bad.

Choose to focus on mentally reminding yourself of your strengths in every situation in which it is appropriate. Positive self-talk is a habit you choose to practice. It is not bragging to yourself. It is simply reminding yourself of your strengths and accomplishments.

Building Self-Confidence

Self-confidence increases as you learn that you can count on yourself. When you commit yourself to something, do it. Develop a reputation with yourself for doing things well. Build self-confidence by selecting challenging goals and reaching them. Ask yourself "What are my reliable strengths?" "How well do I expect to do in challenging situations?"

Developing a Positive Self-Concept

Develop a positive self-concept by spending time writing out positive "I am . . ." statements. Start by observing your self-talk. Make a list of ten "I am" phrases and statements you think or say about yourself. Replace negative statements with positive statements.

Building a Positive Self-Image

A positive self-image is visual. It influences how you dress, your posture, your grooming, how your room looks, places you choose to go, where you expect to work after college, and how your course work looks when you hand it in. Experiment with some of these different aspects of self-image and observe what effects you get.

When all "self" factors are strong you believe in yourself, like yourself, cope well with new challenges, and stay healthy. Also, you'll find the world is a better place for everyone, and people want you to be successful.

WHAT WORKS: SELF-APPRECIATION AND SELF-CRITICISM

The ability to be successful in reaching goals, learning from failures, and having good friends usually requires a balance between self-esteem and self-criticism. It takes a blend of self-confidence and self-doubt. It takes a positive self-image open enough to accept the existence of flaws and weaknesses.

The student who is constantly self-critical without having self-appreciation seldom accomplishes much. The person who is constantly self-appreciating without self-criticism seldom admits to mistakes, weaknesses, and errors in a way that could lead to important learning.

Healthy self-esteem, self-confidence, and a good self-image provide an inner stability that lets you do the things described in the self-assessment list that follows. Which of them is true of you?

Developing Your Inner Resources

In many ways this chapter is an introduction to psychological fitness (covered in more depth in Chapter 15). The main purpose here, however, has been to present useful information about psychological differences between more successful and less successful college students.

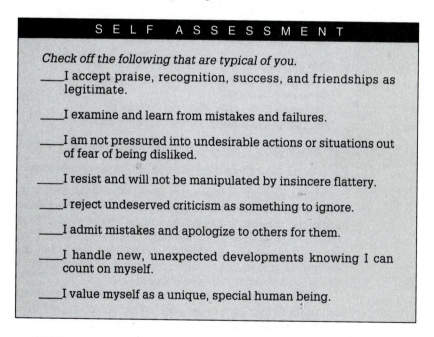

SELF ASSESSMENT

Check off the following that are typical of you.

____I accept praise, recognition, success, and friendships as legitimate.

____I examine and learn from mistakes and failures.

____I am not pressured into undesirable actions or situations out of fear of being disliked.

____I resist and will not be manipulated by insincere flattery.

____I reject undeserved criticism as something to ignore.

____I admit mistakes and apologize to others for them.

____I handle new, unexpected developments knowing I can count on myself.

____I value myself as a unique, special human being.

REMEMBER: All students experience anxiety, tension, self-doubt, failure, nervousness, and uncertainty. The key difference is that the more successful students persist. They keep going. The less successful students give up too easily. They quit when they become frustrated, don't do well at first, or do less well than others.

Students who persist through difficult times have the characteristics found in the list below. Check off the characteristics you have.

___ Able to daydream about possible accomplishments with a mixture of practical positive and negative thinking.

___ Handle the freedom, uncertainty, complexity, and difficulties of college life by being both self-reliant and receptive to guidance.

___ Counteract failure and hurtful criticism with positive self-talk and healthy self-appreciation.

___ Develop self-confidence and a positive self-image through a balance of self-appreciation and self-criticism.

___ Accept nervousness, not doing well at first, and fears as normal feelings.

❏ ACTION GUIDELINES: Feeding Back from the Future

To practice using your imagination in the way that leads to academic achievement, follow these steps:

1. Get a large sheet of paper.

2. At the top write a heading something like
"My 12-Week Success Plan for Fall Term"

3. Fill in four subheadings across the page:
"Feelings I want to enjoy at the end of the term"
"Resources Available"
"Obstacles, Difficulties, Potential Problems"
"Final exam week—How I want it to be for me"

4. In the lower right-hand corner make a space for "Intended GPA."

5. Fill in the blanks by asking yourself the following questions.

Imagine yourself at final exam week. What do you want that week to be like? Do you want to feel well-prepared for your exams? Have all your term papers and projects finished before finals? Have enough time to study? Be rested and relaxed with no late-night cramming? Enter finals with a high grade average already established through midterm exams and other tests? Looking forward to exams with confidence, expecting them to give you a chance to show what you have learned?

Write down how you want things to be during final exam week. Be practical. What do you think is possible? What do you expect that with an effort you have a good chance of accomplishing in the 12 or so weeks between now and finals?

How much would you like to experience feelings of achievement? Pride? Self-confidence? Self-appreciation? Praise and recognition from your friends? Academic honors? Write down your desired feelings under the heading on the left side.

What obstacles lie in your way? What will make it difficult for you to accomplish your desired goals? Start listing these. Be specific. What intermediate goals do you have to reach?

If your list becomes overwhelming, go back to your hopeful list for finals week and modify it downward. Be practical.

What resources are available to you? What information, knowledge, skills, or help do you need? What have you learned from your identification of college resources that might help you be more successful than you first thought? Should you revise your expectations upward?

Take a few days to fill out these four elements in your success plan for the term. After you register for your classes, create a similar plan for each course. Practice imagining yourself as though finals week is now and you feel good about all the things you did during the past weeks so that you feel relaxed, self-confident, and well-prepared.

As you read Part Two in *Student Success* you will get many more practical suggestions on how to succeed in each course and make your plan for the term come true.

SUCCESS GROUP ACTIVITIES

1. Show each other your personal Academic Success Plan for the term. Talk with each other about what effect the activity of outlining the plan has had on you.

2. Discuss the approach to developing your inner resources described in this chapter. What is your reaction to learning that it is desirable to be paradoxical? What does self-esteem mean to each of you? Self-confidence? A positive self-image?

3. Talk with each other about students who seem "most likely to succeed." What are your own observations about why some students are more successful than others? Make a list describing successful students you know. Contrast this with a list describing what less successful students do.

Cover the negative side as well. Are there some ways of being successful in school that are not attractive to you? What disadvantages do you see to being very successful in college? What drawbacks and problems come with being excellent? Discuss why it is normal for all students to feel nervous and anxious, do poorly at times, and have doubts about their abilities.

4. Have each member of your group interview one or two upper classmen who are successful in college in ways that you like. Start with questions such as "What do you do to be successful at this college?" "Can you explain why you are more successful than other students?" Also ask, "What did you wish you had known when you first started here?" Then compare your interview findings.

5. Now that you've finished Part One, devote one session to a review of what you've learned about all the resources available to you. Find out what each person has learned. Be sure to congratulate yourselves on what you've accomplished in such a short time.

OPTIONAL ADVANCED GROUP ACTIVITY

Give each group member a chance to practice expressing both sides of the following:

being excellent in college

self-reliance, coupled with being controlled by external forces

self-appreciation and self-criticism.

Don't pressure anyone to do this. Merely make the group available, if you wish, for a member to practice new ways of thinking and feeling in a safe place with supportive friends.

part two

Time Management: Self-Management

- ❏ *How to Manage a Tight Schedule Successfully*

- ❏ *Setting and Achieving Your Study Goals*

- ❏ *Learning More with Less Time and Effort*

4

How to Manage a Tight Schedule Successfully

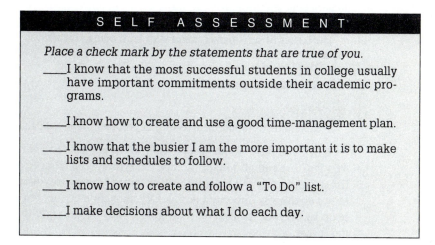

S E L F   A S S E S S M E N T

Place a check mark by the statements that are true of you.

_____I know that the most successful students in college usually have important commitments outside their academic programs.

_____I know how to create and use a good time-management plan.

_____I know that the busier I am the more important it is to make lists and schedules to follow.

_____I know how to create and follow a "To Do" list.

_____I make decisions about what I do each day.

Successful College Students Do More

Success in college is closely related to success in activities outside your academic program. One of the main findings of the study conducted by The College Board was that success in college results from both scholastic achievement and "follow-through" as indicated by "persistent and successful extra-curricular accomplishment."

Students in the study agreed. When they were asked to rate each other on success in college, they picked students who got good grades and "who were also hard-working, well-organized achievers in other areas."

What this means is that your involvement in student government, marching band, symphony, choir, athletics, school newspaper, media productions, church activities, special interest groups, clubs, special campus events, and intramural sports can improve your chances of success in college. The same holds true for working students, adult students, and married students. Active students do better in college.

Why is this so? Why doesn't all this extra activity reduce the chances of success? The answer is that when you have to organize your efforts, avoid wasting time, and do well at the things that really count, you become better at almost everything you do. When the seniors in the College Board study were asked what contributed to a successful and satisfying career in college, 73 percent said the "ability to organize tasks and time effectively."

Time Management Is Self-Management

To accomplish your purposes for being in college and succeed in other important activities, you can't be passive. You must actively control what you do with yourself through conscious choices. In other words, you must do well at managing yourself in the time available to you.

The basics of self-management start with being able to:

1. Set priorities.
2. Not do less important things.
3. Say no.
4. Start and stop specific activities at predetermined times.

When you have major responsibilities in addition to your classes, your "To Do" list can no longer include everything you want to do. Now your list must identify the most important things to do, and you must postpone or not do the less important things. Olympic athletes succeed in making the team by staying focused on their goal. They concentrate their actions on the future.

Your situation may not be of the same magnitude as an Olympic athlete but there is one similarity: You have to manage yourself well or you won't make it.

Self-Management with Lists, Schedules, and Calendars

If you are going to be successful in life, you have to know what you are doing. That statement may seem extraordinarily simple-minded, but it is worth stating. People who don't know what they are doing are rarely successful—at least not consistently.

So the question is, do you know what you are doing? Does what you do each day get you closer to your desired educational goals while you enjoy activities with your friends and fulfill your other commitments? To keep on track, you need effective ways of organizing your self-management plan.

Your Daily List

Get into the habit of making a daily list that combines your scheduled activities and the important things you want to do that day. After listing what you want to do, code the most important items and make sure you give them priority over less important items.

Your Weekly Schedule

To decide what is most important, you need to know your week's schedule. Start each week of the term by making a schedule, using a form such as the ones printed in this book. Fill in all your class times, meetings, important events, study times, exams, practice hours, support group meetings, and so forth. We'll go into this in greater detail in Chapter 5.

Your Term Calendar

How do you know what to fill in on your weekly schedule? At the start of each term, take the syllabus for each course and fill in your calendar for the term. After the first day of classes fill in your calendar with every scheduled exam and due dates for papers, projects, and reports. Fill in all the other important events that occur during the term. Self-management is simple. You decide in advance what is important for you to do, and then you do it.

Who Has Time?

"But I'm too busy. I don't have time to fill in calendars, make weekly schedules, and make To Do lists every day!"

Our response to that statement is that these are self-management procedures essential for the very reason that you don't have enough time for everything. These procedures will help you create the time you need.

> The student who claims not to have enough time to make up the calendar, schedules, and lists is like the man chopping his winter's firewood late in the fall. A couple out walking noticed that he was chopping very hard but not getting much wood cut. When they saw that his axe was dull, they asked, "Why don't you stop and sharpen your axe?" Without pausing in his work, he yelled back, "I can't stop to sharpen my axe, I have too much wood to cut!"

The busier you are, the more essential it is for you to make and use calendars, schedules, and lists. Self-management helps you do what you must do and postpone or say no to the other things. Success in college is not a matter of how much energy you expend or how many hours you spend studying. Success depends on what results you get from your efforts. With a good self-management plan you can get better results in fewer hours than students who don't manage themselves well.

Creating Time from Time You Waste

Wasting time is one of the most enjoyable pastimes known to college students. You should be able to do whatever you wish with your time. But, if you feel that you are losing control of your time and not accomplishing what you want, you might review the following list of time consumers. Our colleague Larry Smith, Vice President for Marketing and Student Affairs at Eastern Michigan University and co-author of *The Instructor's Guide to Student Success,* developed this list by talking to hundreds of students.

Time consumers include:

talking with friends

talking on the telephone, telephone interruptions

daydreaming

watching television

sleeping

listening to music

drop-in visitors

reading (other than school material)

playing sports, games, or hobbies

cleaning room or apartment, doing laundry, grocery shopping, or cleaning desk

"goofing around" or "partying"

eating or snacking

spending too much time in the student center

procrastinating or worrying

Our students have described simple procedures you can use for limiting the amount of time you spend in many of these activities and eliminating those which are of no value. But, before we talk about how you can make these changes, you need to answer two questions, "How much time do I actually have?" and "How much time am I spending wisely and unwisely?" Once you have answered these questions, you'll be able to make more productive use of your time and create time for things you would rather be doing.

How Much Time Do You Really Have?

To prove to yourself that you have more time than you think, take one of the blank weekly schedules we provide in this book. For one week record the time you spend just sitting around, watching television, chatting with friends, and being involved in other activities you enjoy that take time that could be better spent.

After one week, look at your week's record closely. What blocks of time did you waste? What types of activities do you spend your time on that are not really productive? After answering these questions, go a step further. Turn to Chapter 6 and read how to create and follow a weekly schedule. Following the guidelines in that chapter, take a blank schedule and fill it in.

Try following your schedule for a week. Carry it around with you. When you find yourself doing things you want to avoid, look at the schedule and see what you had planned. Then do what you should be doing. Don't make your schedule so rigid you don't have time for any of your old unproductive behavior. Nobody feels comfortable giving up all their old favorites. You are going to make changes slowly. No one follows a schedule to the letter.

Each night take a couple of minutes to go over your schedule to see whether you did the main things you had set out to accomplish. By the end of the week, you'll see the changes that are beginning to take place in your life. You'll be able to scan your chart and know whether you are eliminating some of the old time-wasters and saving some time for those naps, movies, and other things you have been missing.

If you compare your schedule to your previous list, which shows where you were wasting your time, you'll see what you are going to have to give up if you want those naps. It is all up to you.

Do you really want to spend less time doing things you enjoy but are not very productive? Be honest with yourself. Do you find it relaxing to sit around, watch television, and chat with friends? Would you feel you were losing out if you didn't spend time talking to your friends in the next room?

Decide what you are willing to do less of, whether it is reducing your television time or video game action. Next, figure out what it is you would rather be doing. Would you prefer to take a nap after class instead of sitting around talking with friends? Would you be better off going to the library between classes to complete your studying so you'll have time for a concert this weekend?

Time management boils down to deciding what you want from your time. You decide what you are going to eliminate and what you are going to substitute in its place. Then you practice substituting those things from which you'll derive greater pleasure or payoffs for those things that are less important.

Thinking Positively to Take Action

Before getting started with your time management plan, it is important to consider the types of voices which may guide your behavior. As Larry Smith has noted, successful time management is enhanced by becoming aware of two types of voices which often guide our actions. These voices are the "Take Action Now Voices" and the "Do It Later Voices."

Which voices guide your actions most often?

Take Action Now Voices	*Do It Later Voices*
____ Let's get it over with.	____ I don't feel like it now.
____ It's already late.	____ There's still time.
____ You know it, just do it.	____ I'll do it later.
____ They'll be pleased with what I've done.	____ This other thing is more important.
____ It's a challenge.	____ I'll be better prepared later.
____ It'll be fun when I get into it.	____ It may solve itself if I wait.
____ Once I get started it will go quickly.	____ If I wait someone else may do it.
____ If I don't do it now, I'll have to do it later.	____ I need more information.

As you listen to the voices that guide your behavior, you'll discover that a major step to becoming a successful student and person is to recognize and cope with "Do It Later Voices" that hinder your time management. You'll want to consider replacing those voices with "Take Action Now Voices."

Becoming a "Take Action Now" person may be hard work. Once you have developed the habit of letting "Take Action Now Voices" guide your behavior, you'll be in a better mental framework to achieve your goals. You may also find that life is a bit more enjoyable, now that you are getting things done on time and not worrying about what you have been putting off.

Take Control of Your Life

As we said before, the best way to stay in control of your life and your time is to use a weekly chart where you fill in the times you attend class, study, work, take naps, go to a movie, do homework, or do whatever is important. Once you fill in the schedule, you'll have your self-managed time plan for the week ahead.

As you go through the week, keep a record of what you actually do. Don't feel guilty if you don't follow the plan exactly. You are after *experience*. The main thing is to observe how well your self-created weekly time schedule works for you.

Each night and when the week is finished, review how well you used your time. What differences do you see and feel in comparison to your past ways?

As you gain experience, you will find that a weekly schedule only takes five minutes to make and a minute each night to anticipate the day ahead. Once you develop scheduling as a habit, you can be more flexible with it.

When you have more to do in the time available, you can be more effective by being more efficient. Some students with great time pressure don't do as well, however, because they take risky shortcuts. Skipping classes, depending on friends' notes, and buying term papers is risky business. You really don't need risky shortcuts to succeed. By working to acquire efficient and effective time management learning and reading skills, you are using the challenges of college to become a competent person.

The time management tips in *Student Success* can have an immediate impact on your life. You don't have the luxury of putting off your work to a later time. You need to start now to manage your time wisely and use those time management techniques from *Student Success* that will have the biggest payoff.

❏ ACTION GUIDELINES

1. Go to the bookstore and look through the various calendars and weekly and daily schedules for sale. Also look at the personal organizer systems. Some people find them very useful.

If you don't see anything you like, consider creating your own forms and duplicating them at the copy center.

2. If you have a group leader who is using the *Instructor's Manual* that goes with *Student Success*, try using the time management system developed for college students by Larry Smith. The *Instructor's Manual* has blank copies of monthly, weekly, and daily schedules from which you may choose.

3. If time management is a new idea to you, look at several paperback books on the subject. One of the classics is *How to Get Control of Your Time and Your Life* by Alan Lakein. Because it is an older book, you can find copies in used bookstores. A newer time management book specifically for college students is *Studying Smart* by Diana Scharf with Pam Hait.

SUCCESS GROUP ACTIVITIES

1. Tell each other about your experiences using lists, schedules, and calendars. Have you ever made a list of all the things you had to do and then separated the most important from the least important items? What practical tips can you give each other about how to use lists and schedules?

2. Tell each other how you feel about making something you enjoy a low-priority item. Tell each other how you feel about saying no when someone asks you to do something.

3. Now that you've completed a chapter on time management, can you handle the idea that time is an illusion? There is no time in the universe. It doesn't exist outside your mind. Like Einstein said, time is an experience of relative motion, of something happening in relation to the earth spinning around the sun at a fixed rate. Does this perspective help you understand why we emphasize self-management throughout this chapter?

4. Celebrate your accomplishments. Go to a movie, have a party for yourselves, or do something for fun as a group.

5

Setting and Achieving
Your Study Goals

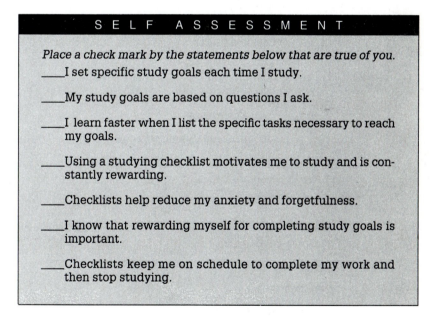

HOW TO SET COURSE AND STUDY GOALS

You need goals to know where you're going in the process of educating yourself. When you know what you want to achieve, you can set your mind to it, achieve it, and stop worrying about whether or not you'll do well in your courses. Setting goals is one of the strongest ways to motivate yourself to study efficiently and effectively.

Students who don't set specific study goals are usually uncertain about *when* they are going to do *what* they have to do in order to do well in their courses. If you can determine what you should study to pass a course and set up a schedule to achieve those goals, you'll be in good shape. Now let's make sure you know how to set study goals and design a schedule to achieve them. We're going to develop a detailed plan for succeeding in each of your courses.

How do I figure out what my study goals should be?

First, you have to ask, "Who or what can tell me what I have to do to learn what I would like to and earn my desired grade in the course?" The best sources of information are listed below.

Put a check mark by those you know you could use more often:

_____ my instructors

_____ assigned course materials

_____ course outlines

_____ course schedules

_____ other students

_____ class discussions

_____ student manuals and programs

From these sources you will usually be able to tell what important tasks you have to accomplish to achieve your desired grade and become a more intelligent person.

What types of tasks are usually required of students who wish to learn a lot and earn good grades?

1. attending class
2. passing tests
3. passing quizzes
4. writing papers
5. participating in class discussions and presentations
6. completing projects

What should I consider when scheduling my study activities?

In addition to knowing the types of tasks that you must accomplish, you should know *how, when,* and *where* they should be accomplished.

What questions should I ask when setting up my study schedule?

Check those which you typically ask.

____ When must each study goal be completed?

____ How much time do I have to complete the specific study goals?

____ How much can I reasonably expect to accomplish between now and the time the assignments are due?

____ How can I divide up my studying so that I don't put everything off until the end?

____ How much should I do each day if I wish to accomplish my specific goals on schedule?

____ Are there specific requirements for the completion of assignments (such as format for papers, number of pages, and style used for references?)

____ How will I be required to demonstrate that I have accomplished the goals?

After answering these questions, you'll be better equipped to design an effective schedule for completing the study tasks that lead to your course assignments and goals. You will know where you are going, how you will get there, and how to recognize when you've arrived.

SCHEDULING TASKS TO ACHIEVE YOUR GOALS

The process of scheduling is quite simple:

1. Determine your goal.
2. Figure out what study tasks you have to perform to achieve your goal and how much time you'll have in which to complete them.
3. Plan to spend specific study periods completing your study tasks.
4. Use a checklist to record your progress as you complete your tasks.

Here's how to set up a schedule to achieve a goal. We'll use a model in which the student's goal is to pass an exam with a score of 90 percent or better. Our student decides that the best way to achieve this goal is to use the technique of collecting and answering questions that are likely to be on the next exam. The steps to take in scheduling and completing tasks that will lead to her goal follow.

Reprinted by permission of UFS, Inc.

Steps in Scheduling

Goal: To receive a grade of 90 percent or better on the next test.

Step 1 Determine when and where the next will be and what material it will cover.

Step 2   Determine the sources of test questions (textbook chapters, lecture notes, study groups, old tests, student manuals, and so on).

Step 3   Determine how many chapters must be read between now and the test.

Step 4   Plan to read a specific number of chapters each week and to develop questions from them.

Step 5   Plan to spend specific study periods each week developing test questions from course notes, old tests, discussion groups, friends, student manuals, and so on.

Step 6   Plan to spend specific study periods each week making and taking practice tests.

Step 7   Design a checklist to record progress in reading chapters, collecting questions and answers, and taking practice tests.

Is all that work really necessary? Isn't there an easier way?

At first glance, you may think it is a lot of work to follow these steps to achieve your study goals. A successful study plan must deal effectively with many difficulties you may face learning and remembering important information. So, yes, there is a lot of work involved in being successful in school. But as we describe in the next section, you will find that your study schedule will help you reach your study goals and actually save you time and make learning much easier.

THE BENEFITS OF RECORDING YOUR PROGRESS

You Keep Yourself on Schedule

Checklists are probably the most effective means of keeping yourself consciously aware of taking the actions that will lead to your goal. You define the tasks that you plan to accomplish, determine when you'll have time to complete them, record when each task is completed, and reward yourself for completing the task on schedule. That's not so hard, and it will have a tremendous motivating effect on your performance.

You Reduce Anxiety and Forgetfulness

We have found that when students keep checklists, they have less anxiety about whether or not they're studying frequently enough. Also, you will find that after establishing a schedule, you will be more likely to study and complete tasks. Your checklists will serve as reminders of what you need to do and when you need to complete it.

You Record and Reward Your Progress

When you use a checklist, you reward yourself for being at places on time and accomplishing specific tasks. Our goal is to help you establish reasonable goals and to accomplish those goals. Using checklists is the best way to record your progress. Checklists will remind you of your responsibilities and accomplishments. Checklists say to you, " This is what you have to do today," or "Congratulations for having accomplished this."

Few students fall by the wayside when they have clear means of establishing goals and of recording and rewarding their progress, provided that they know how to study. If you reward yourself for completing tasks, you'll find that you are more likely to achieve your goals.

IMPORTANT STEPS IN DEVELOPING A CHECKLIST

What things should I include in my checklist?

1. Specify each of the tasks that you must accomplish to achieve your overall goal.

2. Arrange the tasks in order of importance and according to when each is most easily accomplished.

3. Indicate next to each task when you expect to achieve it.

4. Record next to each task the actual date it has been completed.

5. Record next to each task the reward you will give yourself for having accomplished this task.

6. Record whether or not you have rewarded yourself for having accomplished the task on time.

7. Record whether or not you have rewarded yourself for having accomplished the overall goal.

What would a checklist look like for the student whose goal is passing her next test?

Following is an example of what went into developing the student's checklist.

Alexa Shaughnessy
Introductory Psychology
Goal: To receive a passing grade on first psychology
        test of the semester.
Exam date: September 29
Today's date: September 1
Responsibilities: Read Chapters 1-5 in *Understanding*
        Human Behavior: An Introduction to
        Psychology by McConnell and Philipchalk

See how Alexa's checklist looked before she completed her work. Take a minute to look it over before reading on.

Alexa decided to reward herself each time she completed one of her tasks on time. She set due dates, then recorded when each task was completed and whether or not she had received her reward. It was important for her to list her rewards so that there was something to motivate her to complete her tasks on time. Too often in the past, she had found that she put everything off until the last minute and became panic-stricken when she realized how much she had to do. Now, whenever she completed a task on time, she wrote "Yes" on the chart, indicating that she had rewarded herself for doing so.

Alexa listed a series of rewards to choose from whenever she completed a task on time. She was free to choose rewards from outside the list, but was encouraged to develop a list that would motivate her to keep up with her studies.

Alexa's reward list includes:

1.   listen to record

2.   take nap

3.   eat snack

4.   jog

5.   watch television

6.   play video game

7.   watch music video

8.   call boyfriend

9.   ride bike

10.   go to movie

11.   lunch date

12.   read favorite magazine.

Reward for passing test: Party!

Alexa's list of rewards will be different from yours. Perhaps your list would include a back massage or playing cards. Remember, everyone works

Alexa's beginning checklist

Study Behavior	Due Date	Date Completed	Reward	Yes/No
1. Read Chapter 1, and generate questions, answers, and summary	Sept. 2			
2. Read Chapter 2 (same as 1)	Sept. 5			
3. Read Chapter 3 (same as 1)	Sept. 9			
4. Read Chapter 4 (same as 1)	Sept. 16			
5. Read Chapter 5 (same as 1)	Sept. 23			
6. Generate questions from today's lecture and take practice quiz	Sept. 1			
7. Same as 6	Sept. 3			
8. Same as 6	Sept. 5			
9. Same as 6	Sept. 8			
10. Same as 6	Sept. 10			
11. Same as 6	Sept. 12			
12. Same as 6	Sept. 15			
13. Same as 6	Sept. 17			
14. Same as 6	Sept. 19			
15. Same as 6	Sept. 22			
16. Same as 6	Sept. 24			
17. Same as 6	Sept. 26			
18. Generate questions from old test	Sept. 10			
19. Make up and take practice test for Chapters 1, 2	Sept. 7			
20. Make up and take practice test for Chapters 3, 4	Sept. 17			
21. Make up and take practice test for Chapter 5	Sept. 24			
22. Make up and take practice test from all sources of questions	Sept. 27 & 28			
23. Meet with study group to make up practice test	arrange			
24. Take exam	Sept. 29			
25. Achieve goal: Pass Exam				

for rewards that he or she values. We encourage you to reward yourself for studying effectively, just as most people reward themselves for going to work by collecting pay checks.

Isn't it rather time-consuming to make checklists? Couldn't the time be better spent by studying?

The checklist took Alexa ten minutes to write. Once it was completed, she knew what she had to do and when she had to complete each task. Afterward, she spent less time worrying about whether or not she was doing the right things and whether she was ahead of or behind schedule. The checklist was an excellent investment in learning to study efficiently and effectively. You may use any type of checklist you wish. This one is simply a model with which our students have had much success.

Benefits of Developing a Checklist

What can you guarantee the checklist will do?

The checklist of specific things to do is very helpful. If you have everything written out in an organized fashion, it is easy to refer to. You can see what needs to be done more easily. You won't be overwhelmed by the amount of information you need to learn. Also, you are much less likely to be surprised by an important test or paper.

First, if Alexa follows her checklist, she will have a good set of questions, answers, and summaries for each chapter. *Second*, she will not be faced with the problem of having put off reading the chapters until just before the exam. She will study the chapters periodically over a month and will finish them at least a week before the test. *Third*, she will make up questions and answers immediately following her lectures and will practice quizzing herself to prove that she really comprehends the lectures.

Fourth, Alexa will take a practice test for each chapter before she takes a final practice test. Before the exam she will be well-prepared and will have spent less time in final review. This change has a tremendous positive effect on most students' digestive tracts and fingernails. Stomachs and fingers often take a beating when students wait until the last minute to figure out what will be on the next exam.

Fifth, Alexa will find out from other students in the course what they think will most likely be on the exam. *Sixth*, she will also obtain a fair idea of what will be on this year's exam by looking at a copy of last year's exam. *Seventh*, she will be constantly reminded whether she was ahead of, keeping up with, or behind her study schedule. *Eighth*, she may get encouragement and recognition from her success group partners. *Ninth*, she will reward herself for completing each of the tasks leading to her goal of passing the exam.

Finally, Alexa will increase her motivation to study. In fact, in talking about this schedule, she became so enthusiastic that she was going to do the first two chapters immediately to get a head start. We suggested to her, however, "Don't let yourself jump ahead; only allow yourself to study for a certain amount of time. When you've finished, reward yourself, and go on to something else."

Alexa's Completed Checklist

It is interesting to compare the proposed checklist that Alexa had made out at the beginning of the month with the same checklist after she had attempted to follow her schedule of tasks and to reward herself for completing the tasks on time. As you will see, she chose most of her rewards from her original list. Periodically she satisfied a whim or spur-of-the-moment desire that she hadn't included on her original list of rewards. It is important to notice that she did not have to spend a lot of money to reward herself. By choosing activities that she enjoyed but seldom found time for when going to school, she was able to encourage and reward her good study behavior while keeping herself out of debt.

Many students ask, "But what can I reward myself with? Everything costs so much." Yet students often complain that they never have time to do things they enjoy—playing cards, watching television, riding their bikes, and going out with friends. Scheduling rewards for completing tasks encourages students to partake of their favorite activities. They have no reason to feel guilty, as so many students do when they take time away from their studies. The rule of thumb is *when you earn a reward for studying, take it, and never, never, cheat yourself.*

Notice that Alexa failed on several occasions to complete her tasks on time. Therefore, she did not reward herself. It was important that she receive the reward only when the task had been completed on time because procrastination had been a big problem for her in the past. She decided it was important that her chart serve as a means of encouraging her not only to complete her work but also to complete work on time.

For other students, punctuality may not be a problem. It would not be necessary to only reward themselves if their tasks were finished on time. But, we usually find that if a person begins skipping tasks or finishing tasks later than he had planned, he tends to return to less effective study techniques, like cramming before exams.

REWARDING YOUR PROGRESS

The Importance of Rewards

It is human to try to escape from or avoid adverse situations. Students want to take the pressure off themselves, finish reading the stupid book, get the test over with, and keep from flunking out or doing poorly. In our estimation, this attitude is tragic. Students can enjoy going to school.

Alexa's completed checklist

Study Behavior	Due Date	Date Completed	Reward	Yes/No
1. Read Chapter 1, and generate questions, answers, and summary	Sept. 2	Sept. 2	Hour T.V.	Yes
2. Read Chapter 2 (same as 1)	Sept. 5	Sept. 5	Hour T.V.	Yes
3. Read Chapter 3 (same as 1)	Sept. 9	Sept. 9	Read Mags.	Yes
4. Read Chapter 4 (same as 1)	Sept. 16	Sept. 16	Sundae	Yes
5. Read Chapter 5 (same as 1)	Sept. 23	Sept. 23	Hour T.V.	Yes
6. Generate questions from today's lecture and take practice quiz	Sept. 1	Sept. 1	Hour Nap	Yes
7. Same as 6 (*late*)	Sept. 3	Sept. 4	none	no
8. Same as 6	Sept. 5	Sept. 5	Cards	Yes
9. Same as 6	Sept. 8	Sept. 8	Rode bike	Yes
10. Same as 6 (*late*)	Sept. 10	Sept. 11	none	no
11. Same as 6	Sept. 12	Sept. 12	Ice cream	Yes
12. Same as 6 (*late*)	Sept. 15	Sept. 16	none	no
13. Same as 6	Sept. 17	Sept. 17	Tennis	Yes
14. Same as 6	Sept. 19	Sept. 19	Walk	Yes
15. Same as 6	Sept. 22	Sept. 22	Cards	Yes
16. Same as 6	Sept. 24	Sept. 24	Call Friend	Yes
17. Same as 6	Sept. 26	Sept. 26	Hour T.V.	Yes
18. Generate questions from old test	Sept. 10	Sept. 10	Sundae	Yes
19. Make up and take practice test for Chapters 1, 2	Sept. 7	Sept. 7	Show	Yes
20. Make up and take practice test for Chapters 3, 4	Sept. 17	Sept. 17	Show	Yes
21. Make up and take practice test for Chapter 5	Sept. 24	Sept. 24	Show	Yes
22. Make up and take practice test from all sources of questions	Sept. 27 & 28	Sept. 27, 28	3 hours T.V.	Yes
23. Meet with study group to make up practice test	arrange	Sept. 27	Nap	Yes
24. Take exam	Sept. 29	Sept. 29	Date	Yes
25. Achieve goal: Pass Exam	Exam Grade	92 %	Concert	Yes

Student Success will show you many study strategies that will make your studying more enjoyable. We would like to increase your enjoyment of studying and doing well in school by encouraging you to reward yourself for accomplishing tasks and achieving goals.

Students often say "Well, isn't rewarding myself bribery? Why should I reward myself for something I have to do?" The answer is simple: You're more likely to do what's good for you when you encourage yourself to do it. We suggest rewarding yourself with free time—for television, reading magazines, or whatever you enjoy. The rewards need not cost anything. Rewards may simply be opportunities to participate in activities that you enjoy. Go ahead and give yourself periodic rewards for accomplishing tasks.

GUIDELINES FOR USING PROGRESS RECORDS, CHECKLISTS, AND REWARDS

Okay. I'll give these strategies a try. Are there any special rules I should follow in using them?

Yes. We suggest, *first*, that you always *post* your schedules, checklists, and progress records where they will be highly visible. When constantly visible, they will serve as constant reminders of what you should be doing and how well you are doing it.

Second, ask yourself what you should really be able to do in the amount of time you have to accomplish your goal. *Schedule* your work, as suggested earlier, so that all the work for a particular course isn't crammed into a short period of time. Spread your work out. Give yourself time to relax before the test or the date your paper is due.

Third, list the rewards that you will receive for accomplishing your goals. Always reward yourself as you accomplish your goals! Never cheat yourself!

Fourth, show your success team partners how well you are doing. The response from our students throughout the years to checklists, schedules, and progress records has been exceedingly favorable. Students have enjoyed the benefits of having more predictable study schedules. Needless to say, students also enjoyed their rewards. Equally important, students have seen improvements in how much they have learned and in their grades. If you'd like the same results, we encourage you to give these tactics a try.

WHERE WE ARE

Scheduling your tasks and recording and rewarding your progress will be important to your success. You now have specific guidelines about practical strategies to organize your time and energies for successful learning. Chapter 6 will focus on the psychological factors that affect your success in managing your time and work. Once you have completed Chapter 6, you'll be ready to develop a sound plan for scheduling your course work and managing your time.

❏ **ACTION GUIDELINES: Develop a Checklist for One Course**

Take a few minutes to develop a checklist and schedule for accomplishing a goal in one course. Try following the important steps listed for developing a checklist. It will be helpful to review the model checklist on page 56 to develop a sense of what you might include in your own list.

It is important that you start small. By starting out with a checklist for one major task in one course, you will become comfortable with using checklists. Once you have finished Chapter 6, you will be ready to develop a complete time management and scheduling system for all of your course work.

❏ **ACTION REVIEW: Checklist for Success in Setting and Achieving Your Study Goals**

Mark the following statements which are true of you and place an asterisk by those which you will try to develop.

____ I set grade goals for each course.

____ I set specific study goals for each course.

____ I set up a schedule to achieve study goals.

____ I record my progress at achieving study goals.

____ When I achieve study goals, I reward myself.

❏ **ACTION GUIDELINES: Form a Test-Passing Group**

Ask several students in one of your courses to form a study group. Ask them to develop a study goal, schedule, or checklist similar to the list on page 56. Arrange to get together to exchange practice questions and quiz each other as you go through the course.

SUCCESS GROUP ACTIVITIES

1.   Have some fun comparing and developing your personal lists of rewards for reaching your study goals. If you want to, include several rewards that you can get from each other, for example, trading compact discs or VHS movies.

2.   Compare your ideas for developing study goal checklists. Discuss each person's plan for using the checklist during a course.

6

Learning More with Less Time and Effort

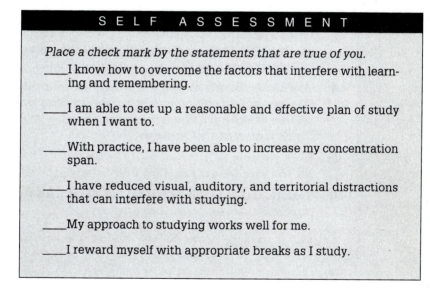

Learning about Learning and Memory

Have you ever felt frustrated during an exam because you can't quite remember something that you know you studied? This chapter will show you strategies that will help you do much better. First, let's look at some problems you may face as you try to learn and remember important material.

Years of research by psychologists have established that the following factors interfere with learning and remembering:

1. Information can't be remembered when it isn't learned well.

2. Recognizing information you have read is not the same as learning information that you can recall. Recognition is the easiest learning; recall is the most difficult.

3. You don't learn or retain information well if you are distracted. Noise, television, music, and people talking all divert part of your brain's attention from what you are studying. Being preoccupied or worried can also distract you from learning and remembering.

4. Information does not transfer from short-term memory to long-term memory without effort, repetition, and practice.

5. Your memory of information lasts longer when learning is spread out over a period of time.

6. Your ability to remember information drops very sharply following the learning. Although the main points of a morning lecture may be recalled while talking to a friend at lunch, much of what was learned will be forgotten two weeks later. Only a small percentage of information is retained if you do not use it or practice relearning it.

7. Trying to learn too much information too fast interferes with accurate recall. Your nervous system needs time to assimilate new learning before taking in more.

8. Information recently learned will be interfered with by similar information learned soon after. This is a process called *retroactive inhibition,* in which you have difficulty recalling new information too similar to other new information.

9. When you have an emotional dislike for the material being learned, you will have difficulty recalling it objectively and accurately.

10. Your learning and remembering are less efficient when you lack interest in the material or motivation to learn.

Knowledge about the factors that can interfere with learning and remembering can help you develop strategies to learn more in less time and with less effort. This chapter will focus on the factors which enhance and hinder your learning and management of time.

Study Regularly

Many freshman students act as though being a successful student is different from being a successful musician with the Chicago Symphony Orchestra, a running back with the Detroit Lions, or a New York stockbroker. Few people would question that to be a successful musician, athlete, or business person you need to practice your profession regularly.

One of the most helpful insights for many students is that to be successful you have to treat college like a job. These students accept the reality that to succeed in college you need to study almost every day and do more studying than you did in high school.

This line of thought only makes sense. Can you imagine the conductor of an orchestra saying to its members, "Our next concert is three weeks away. Let's get together the night before the concert and we'll practice for seven hours." Or, how about the football coach saying to the team, "Guys, to prepare for next Saturday's game, we'll practice 14 hours on Friday. Until then, have fun and get ready for a real workout!"

To do well at anything, you've got to practice frequently for reasonable periods of time. *Too much practice too late will make you a physical and psychological wreck.*

Like any professional, you need a regular training schedule. As a professional student, you need a study schedule that allows you time to learn everything you need to know at a pace that helps your learning settle in and stick with you for years to come.

Some students really believe they can learn just as much by cramming all their studying into a few intense study periods before an exam. If you believe this, ask yourself, "Can I bake a cake faster by turning the oven up to 500 degrees? Can I make a garden grow faster by constantly flooding it with water and surrounding it with heat lamps?" No.

The same holds true for your learning. That's why your courses are scheduled over several months rather than being crammed into one intensive week of study. Studying for brief periods on a regular basis will lead to better learning than if you try to cram all your studying into a couple of longer periods before an exam.

Most of your courses will require constant preparation and review. As we have noted, some students seem to think that since they may have only a few tests in each course, most of their studying can be done within a week before the test. Last minute cramming tends to have fatal consequences.

Getting yourself into the habit of keeping up in each course may be difficult for you, especially if you have a couple of courses that are more demanding than the others. You'll be tempted to spend most of your time on the difficult courses and let the so-called easy courses slide. This is another fatal error.

For years college instructors have been telling students that they need to spend two hours studying outside of class for each hour they spend in class. The truth is that you'll need to spend more time for some classes and less time for other classes.

What it all boils down to is that you need to do the reading and assignments for each class on a regular basis. You want to keep up with each class. You don't want to have that lingering fear that you may be commiting academic suicide by letting one class slide until the last minute. Let's look at how you can set up a reasonable schedule.

SET UP YOUR SCHEDULE

As we've said before, one of your greatest aids will be to use and follow a time schedule. Obtain a month-by-month calendar with spaces that you can fill in with important dates and obligations—when examinations will take place and when papers and projects are due. Next, fill in all the times that you plan to go to concerts, shows, family gatherings, meetings, trips, and so on.

After developing a picture of your major commitments for the months ahead, you are now ready to make up a weekly schedule of your classes, study hours, and other obligations. A weekly schedule gives you a clear picture of what you are doing with your time; it helps you spot an extra hour or two during the day that you can use for studying or other responsibilities. This way you can plan more free evenings to do what you want.

S E L F   A S S E S S M E N T

The following steps for effective scheduling are those upon which most successful academic time-management plans are built. Check off the steps you believe are most important for you.

_____Establish a well-defined and reasonable schedule, one that I can live with.

_____Budget my time to prepare for each class and all my examinations.

_____Budget my time to take care of all of my other personal responsibilities.

_____Study my course notes as soon as possible after each class period, rather than waiting until the last few days before my exams.

_____Give my difficult subjects preferred times with the fewest possible interruptions and disturbances.

_____Reserve time for leisure activities and make sure that I do not study during these periods.

_____Stick to my schedule and reward myself for having achieved my study goals in the allotted time.

A Schedule That Will Work for You

A good schedule will motivate you. Knowing that you have an hour on Thursday morning reserved for studying mentally prepares you to spend that hour doing the studying.

REMEMBER: Do not allow yourself to study too much! Schedule time for the other things that you want to do and stick to your schedule. Many students become so involved in their studying when they first start using the strategies in this book that they keep right on studying through their scheduled breaks. Don't let yourself do this. When you reach the scheduled time to stop, go get some exercise or do whatever you want to do. *Learn how to make yourself stop studying.*

For many students, the problem is not studying too little, the problem is that they study so much they are inefficient in their studying habits.

How Much Time Do You Really Need?

One of Parkinson's Laws is that "work expands to fill available time." You may have experienced this phenomenon in regard to a project such as washing and waxing your car. Let's say that you had three hours available on Saturday morning. If you have three hours available, it will probably take you three hours to get the job done. But let's also say that before you can finish the job, you receive a telephone call informing you that some very special people want you to drive over and pick them up. You would probably, in that circumstance, be able to wash and wax your car to your satisfaction in less than an hour. The approach that we suggest in this book is that you decide what has to be done, do it, and then stop.

Developing Your Own Schedule

Using a weekly study schedule will show you that you have many more hours during the day than you might have realized. You will find blank copies of the weekly schedules at the back of the book. Feel free to tear the schedules out and use them as you wish. After finishing Part Two on time-management (Chapters 4, 5, and 6), you can go on to develop your own weekly schedule. First, look over several weekly schedules of other students to give you an idea of what you might want to include in your own schedule.

In the next few pages, you will find schedules of a college freshman who has no work or athletic obligations, a student-athlete, and a student who has a part-time job. These weekly schedules will show you the types of activities a student can plan for on a weekly basis.

WHAT DO YOU OBSERVE?

Before reading further, take a minute to review the schedule of Mark, a non-working student. As your review the schedule, ask yourself, "What scheduling strategies is Mark using that will improve his learning and memory?" List them on the following page:

1.

2.

3.

4.

5.

Mark's Scheduling Strategies for Improving His Learning and Memory

Notice how Mark prepares for each class by reading ahead in his textbooks. During his reading sessions, he writes out questions he would like to have answered in class.

After class he reviews his lecture notes and writes exam questions. The few minutes after class is the best and easiest time to complete the day's lecture notes. Waiting even a few hours makes it more difficult to remember what certain terms or words meant.

What doesn't show are the many brief time periods during the week when Mark can sit down for five or ten minutes and review notes, write questions, or update his "To Do" list.

At lunch, he usually meets with his success group partner or partners. There they talk about what is happening and show each other what they are doing.

His evening study schedule is now a planned mix of all his subjects. In his first attempt at a study schedule he reserved one evening for each subject. That proved to be inefficient and didn't get good results. Now, by alternating subjects every hour or so, he learns the material more quickly and more accurately.

Mark's schedule reflects his personal aims. He wants to have Saturday and Sunday free, he wants to watch Monday Night Football, he wants time for working out and running, and he wants Friday and Saturday evenings free for parties, dates, and movies.

The point is that Mark's schedule suits Mark. Your own schedule may be much different. This is merely a demonstration to show how you can be in control of your week. First fill in your monthly calendars to lay out the term. Your calendar helps you create your weekly schedule. Then your weekly schedule provides the basis for your daily "To Do" list.

Now review the schedules of a student-athlete and a working student for examples of how different schedules can be for different students.

CONCENTRATE WHILE STUDYING

The key to concentrating effectively is to set a goal for yourself. People who concentrate well focus on achieving a goal they have set. If you decide to study for an hour, ask yourself, "What is my goal for the hour? What will I focus on learning and accomplishing during the hour? Am I going to read a chapter and

Example: Mark's schedule

HOUR	Sunday	Monday	Tuesday	Wednesday	Thursday	Friday	Saturday
7–8		Read					
8–9	Sun. list	Bio & English	Library Read	Read Bio, English	Library Read &	Read Bio, English	Sat. list
9–10		Biology	Study Art	Biology	Study Art	Biology	Basketball
10–11	Church	English	Art	English	Art	English	
11–12		Review Notes	Review Notes	Review Notes	Review Notes	Review Notes	
12–1			Lunch with Friends				
1–2		Psych		Psych		Psych	
2–3		Library	P.E.	Review Notes	P.E.	Review Notes	
3–4	Work-out		Bio. Lab	Work-out	Run	Work-out	
4–5					Success Group		
5–6		Run					
6–7	Success Group		Library	Library	Library		
7–8		Mon. night Football	Eng.	Psych. Study Group	Bio. Study Group	Movie or	Party or
8–9	Laundry		Bio.	Eng.	Psych.	Date	Date
9–10			Psych	Bio.	Eng.		
10–11	Schedule week Mon. list	Tue. list	Wed. list	Th. list	Fri. list		
11–12							

Example: Student athlete schedule

HOUR	Sunday	Monday	Tuesday	Wednesday	Thursday	Friday	Saturday
7–8		←——————— Breakfast ———————→					
8–9	Sleep	English 125		English 125		English 125	
9–10	Breakfast	Speech 100	P.E. 100	Speech 100	P.E. 100	Speech 100	
10–11	Church	P.E. 110	Library	P.E. 110	Library		Game
11–12		Psych 171	Library	Psych 171	Library	Psych 171	
12–1	←——————— Lunch ———————→						
1–2	←— Movies, Taping, and Treatment —→						Day
2–3							
3–4	Relax	Practice					
4–5	Dinner						Dinner
5–6	Relax						
6–7		Dinner					
7–8		Library / or				Relax	
8–9		Study Table					
9–10							
10–11		Sleep					relax
11–12							

Example: Working student schedule

HOUR	Sunday	Monday	Tuesday	Wednesday	Thursday	Friday	Saturday
7–8		*Work —*		*Dorm*			
8–9				*Cafeteria*			
9–10		Math 105	Library	Math 105	Library	Math 105	*Errands*
10–11		German 201	German 201	German 201	German 201		
11–12		Psych 444		Psych 444	Library	Psych 444	
12–1		*Work — Dorm*					*Band*
1–2		*Cafeteria*					
2–3		History 191	Laundry	History 191	Library	History 191	
3–4	History*	Library	Laundry		Library		
4–5	History*	*Marching Band*					*Relax*
5–6		*Practice*					
6–7		*Dinner*					
7–8	Math*	History	Math*	History	Math	*Relax*	
8–9	German*	German*	German*	German*	History*		
9–10	Psych*	German*	Psych*	German*	Psych*		
10–11							
11–12		*Sleep*					

*Library Study

answer eight questions about it? Am I going to solve eight calculus problems? Am I going to write an outline for my paper and start the introduction?" Good concentration requires that you set a goal, focus on it, and work to achieve it.

Eliminate Distractions

Studying at Home

More than likely, your family, roommates, or friends have habits and attitudes that interfere with good studying. These people may have no idea that their behavior bothers you. In contrast, some people will bother you just to get your attention, especially young children.

Let's think of the situations that typically distract students. While you're studying, someone turns on the TV in the next room. You say, "Please don't turn on the TV, it bothers me." The person says, "I'll keep it low." Someone else walks in and wants to talk or needs to be driven to a friend's house. There is a never-ending barrage of interruptions.

So how do you create a peaceful study atmosphere? If you are like many people, you start out by pleasantly asking people not to bother you. If that doesn't work you may act angry. Often that doesn't work. You may even try to enforce some rules regarding your study time. You may designate the area in which you are studying off limits or a quiet area. Then you try to enforce the rules of "Be quiet and leave me alone!" We would suggest another approach. Here's why.

"Quiet hours" in residence halls and in people's homes are often failures. The minute you make rules requiring people to keep noise down or leave you alone, some people seem to go out of their way to demonstrate that the rules can be broken. If you shout, scream, or demand that people keep the noise down you probably won't get the desired results. Even calm rule enforcement can lead to ruffled feathers and headaches. Rule enforcement requires time, which you simply don't need to waste. If you try to enforce rules and people break them, instead of studying you're uptight and furious at what is occurring.

There is a better approach to changing the behavior and attitudes of people around you: *Ask your friends or family for what you want!* Think about what is reasonable and possible; then ask for it. Be clear and specific, and explain in detail exactly what you would like to have from them. You may be surprised at how understanding and supportive people can be.

Remember, you may be asking the people around you to behave quite differently from what they're used to. Their behavior isn't likely to change dramatically overnight. Be patient. Track positives. Notice and appreciate any slight improvement in the direction that you are encouraging. It's up to you to express your appreciation whenever people cooperate. Also, let the people share in your progress.

If you have a friend or family member who is not cooperative, develop a plan for yourself so that you can study and do your course work. Avoid feeling victimized. Instead, come up with a creative plan that will let you continue getting the education you want. Only use strict rule enforcement as a last resort. Remember, your aim is to minimize the amount of time and energy taken away from your real interest, that of studying and learning.

Visual Distractions

Benita is like most students. She has created a comfy nest for herself in her study area. As she closes the door to the den, the wonderful family pictures covering one wall draw her attention. Benita takes several minutes to gaze nostalgically at the photos of herself and Bill at the ocean. The next thing she knows, she's ready to pull out the slides and not bother with studying. Walking to her desk, she spots a pile of magazines she hasn't had a chance to read. There's the TV in the corner. Why not turn it on and catch the last half of the special she wanted to watch? "I can read and watch TV at the same time," she thinks to herself. Everything in the room has a pull for Benita. She feels as though magnetic forces are drawing her to every item in the room.

And that's the trouble. Before she knows it, 20 minutes have slipped away. She glances at the clock and suddenly thinks, "Why have I wasted so much time? Okay. I'll get to work. That's the last time I'll get distracted." That's what she thinks.

As Benita returns to her studies, her mind is distracted from her notes. The family photo on the desk keeps catching her eye. The phone reminds her of several calls she has to make. She starts worrying, "If I don't make those calls tonight, I'll have real problems next week." Before she knows it, she has blown another 15 minutes rehearsing the phone calls that she should be making. Pictures, telephones, magazines, and television programs, constantly distract her from studying.

Minimizing Your Visual Distractions

Your Desk and Chair

If you study at your desk, try to keep it as free of distractions as possible. Once it is cleared off, you won't miss what is gone. Don't go berserk and carry the principle too far. We're not suggesting you create a monastic cell with nothing but bare walls and a small light at your desk. What we suggest is that you sit at a desk or in a chair which is comfortable and free of articles that carry memories, free of articles that cry out, "Pick me up, play with me, use me, gaze at me."

Try placing your desk so that you face a wall that is void of your family history and photos. A blank wall in front of you prevents your eyes from leaving the pages of your notes or text. Place your chair so that you are not looking out a window at the passing scene. Your chair can easily face an area that will not distract you.

Lighting

To reduce eye strain, your room should be well lit, with the main light source off to one side. A light directly behind or in front of you will be reflected from the glossy pages of your textbooks. A constant glare tires your eyes more quickly than indirect lighting. If you can't shift the lamp, shift your desk. Place the desk so that no portion of the bulb shines directly into your eyes. A strong light source pulls your eyes toward it. The constant strain of trying to avoid looking at the light causes eye fatigue.

Spend a few minutes arranging your study environment. There's no use in feeling uncomfortable. The few minutes you spend will save you hours of distracted study and constant mumbling and grumbling: "I just can't get a thing done. I just can't keep my eyes on the pages. I keep thinking of a thousand other things. And my eyes are killing me!" All of these distractions needn't get in your way if you design your study area to encourage studying and not daydreaming. You need to have the best study area possible.

Auditory Distractions

As we noted, "quiet hours" rarely work as well as the rule makers hope. Distracting sounds still interrupt studying. Doors slam, phones ring, horns honk, and people move around. In fact, the quieter the study areas, the more distracting these sounds become.

Steady background sounds can mask distracting noises. Play your radio or stereo softly while you study to create a steady background of "noise" to mask occasional sounds. Experiment with stations or records until you find what works best for you. FM radio stations playing instrumental music are usually best. Talk shows and fast-talking disc jockeys are usually worse for concentration than nothing at all. Some people say that turning on their hair dryers helps them to study. One student reported that he turns his radio to a place where there is no program. The static keeps him from being distracted.

Don't try to study with the television on. If you want to watch a program, watch it. But don't try to avoid feeling guilty by having your book open to read during commercials. Studying with your television on is academic suicide. Use television time as a reward. After you have completed a successful study period, say to yourself, "I've earned a reward. I'll watch television."

Territorial Distractions

If you need to escape from distractions, *go to your favorite library!* Libraries have been designed to help you succeed. People can't yell at you. Your friends can't ask you for attention. Your girlfriend can't bother you with her phone conversation. Your boyfriend won't have "Monday night football" blaring. Your roommate can't drag you into a conversation. Only you can prevent yourself from studying in the library. The obvious exception is the nitwit who sits across from you talking to his girlfriend or tapping his pencil. With minor exceptions, most places in a library are good for studying.

When you first go into a library to find a good spot to study, allow yourself a little warm-up time. Whenever you enter a new territory, your senses are drawn to the environment. You automatically scan new surroundings. You check the walls, floor, and ceiling. You look at the lights, decorations, and furnishings. You look at the people, wonder about certain sounds, and spend time adjusting to the feeling of a new chair. Every time you go to a new place to study, you check out the surroundings before you settle down to work. To improve your efficiency, pick one spot and always try to study there. Studying in the same spot will shorten your warm-up time and allow you to concentrate better.

If your library is a campus social center, try to find a spot with the least amount of people traffic. Find a remote table or desk where you won't be tempted to watch all the action.

ACCEPT YOUR HUMANNESS

Concentration Span

Brent is a sophomore engineering major. During the summer he decided that when he came back to college, he would study three hours every night *without interruption.* He put a sign on his door:

> THE <u>CLOSED</u> DOOR MEANS
> I WANT YOU TO INTERRUPT ME. . .
> **NOT**!

Is he studying more? Yes and no. He can make his body sit at his desk for several hours at a time, but he has a problem that he hardly knows exists. While his eyes look at his book, his mind takes breaks. He sometimes reads several pages and then realizes that he has no idea of what he has read. He has been daydreaming while reading.

Does Brent need more willpower? No. He needs to accept the idea that he is a human being. He needs to accept the idea that there are limitations on what the human mind can be expected to do.

The way to make studying easier is to start with what you can do now and build on that. On the average, how long can you study before your mind slips off to something else? Twenty-five minutes? Ten minutes? Most students can concentrate on a textbook 10 to 15 minutes before they start to daydream.

The next time you study, keep a note pad on your desk and notice approximately how long you can read your textbooks or notes before you start to daydream. Don't set any particular goals for yourself yet. First, find out what is the typical amount of time you can read textbook material before your mind starts to wander. Say that you find your average concentration span is about 12 minutes. Now the question is, what would you like it to be—30 minutes, or perhaps, 45 minutes?

Whatever goal you set for yourself, make certain you allow for your humanness. Be realistic. Set a goal that you can reach with reasonable effort and give yourself enough time to reach it. As a rough guideline, you might aim for a time span of 15 minutes by the end of your freshman year, 25 minutes in your sophomore year, 35 minutes in your junior year, and 45 minutes in your senior year. Graduate students should be able to study for about an hour without losing their concentration.

MANDATORY BREAKS

Once you determine your concentration span, set up your study schedule so that you take a brief break after each study segment and a long break about once an hour. If you do, you will find that you can start and return to your studies much more easily than before.

In fact, you will find the end of a study segment coming so quickly you will be tempted to continue. *Don't do it*. Keep your agreement with yourself. When you promise to take a quick break after 12 minutes, do so. Do not allow yourself to study more than the allotted time.

A look at the records of most students shows why it is necessary to take these breaks even when they don't want to. With segmented study hours, studying is easier than expected, but after a while the old ways of studying creep back in.

What happens? The critical point comes when you reach the end of a study segment and find yourself so interested in the material that you decide to keep on. If you do, your mind seems to say, "I can't trust you. You promised me a break after each 14 minutes, but after I fulfilled my part, you kept me working."

When you promise your mind a break after 12 or 14 minutes, *keep your word!* No matter how much you want to continue, make yourself take a short break. Get up and stretch. Get a drink of water or a breath of fresh air before starting the next study segment.

❏   ACTION GUIDELINES: Learning about Learning and Memory

1.   Read the sections on memory and forgetting in several different introductory psychology textbooks.
2.   Make a list of all the principles and factors that help or hinder learning and memory.
3.   Look through *Student Success* to see how it is organized to use the knowledge of these facts and principles.
4.   List several techniques you could use on a regular basis to improve your memory.
5.   Get together with some other students who are motivated to do well in college and talk about what you have learned from this information about learning and memory.

❏   ACTION GUIDELINES: Setting Up a Schedule

At the back of this book you will find schedules that can be removed. Tear out the first schedule and use the suggestions in Chapters 4, 5, and 6 to create a weekly schedule to manage your time.

Post your schedule where you will be able to see it. As you complete the activities during the week, cross off each square that represents that activity.

By keeping track of the activities you complete, you are likely to find that you are motivated to stay on schedule. Notice that you are not being encouraged to schedule your entire life. Just schedule the activities that you have to complete for your academic and personal satisfaction.

Make sure you leave time for just doing what you please and for all those spontaneous activities that make life so rewarding. At the end of the week, review your schedule to determine the percentage of activities you have completed. If you feel you have done well in keeping to your schedule, give yourself a little reward.

❏   ACTION REVIEW: Checklist for Learning More with Less Effort

Use the list below to review how well you are managing your learning effort. Some students place this list on their wall or in a conspicuous place to remind them how to manage their daily learning.

___ Have I outlined a weekly study schedule for myself?

___ Do I write out and follow daily time schedules?

___ Have I asked people to be considerate of my need to study?

___ Is my study free of distractions?

___ Do I mask distracting sounds with soft music or some other steady background noise?

___ Have I arranged good lighting?

___ Do I study in the same place each time?

___ Do I avoid studying one subject too long?

___ Have I determined my concentration span and set up study segments geared to my present ability?

___ Do I take short breaks after study segments and a long break each hour?

___ Have my grades improved as a result of using these scheduling and management strategies?

❏ **ACTION GUIDELINES: Quiet Roommates**

One of the most important supports any college student can have is his or her roommate. However, too often roommates inadvertently create distractions for one another. Rather than wait to complain when your roommate creates auditory and visual distractions that drive you up the wall, take a few minutes to have a frank discussion first. Ask him or her what conditions the two of you can create so that you can both accomplish your studying.

It will help to be as honest as possible. If you can't stand hearing rock music, even playing softly, when you are trying to read, say so. Even if you regularly study in the library, you'll periodically work in your room. Agree with your roommate what will and will not go on during studying.

Don't forget to be human. Both you and your roommate will break the rules now and then. Laugh it off. Make a joke about the distraction. Everyone tests rules. Once you and your roommate adjust to one another's study needs, you'll have reduced one of the greatest sources of conflict that typically develop between roommates.

SUCCESS GROUP ACTIVITIES

1. Compare your weekly schedules. Support each other in creating a schedule that is personally suitable. Does one person prefer to get up early and start studying at 6:00 a.m.? Does another prefer to sleep late and study until midnight or 1:00 a.m.?

2.   Compare samples of your daily "To Do" lists. Talk with each other about how well it is working to set priorities and do only the most important things each day.

3.   Talk about the principles affecting learning and remembering listed at the beginning of the chapter. What effects have this chapter and the ACTION GUIDELINES on learning about learning had on you?

part three

How to Get "A's" Without Getting Stressed Out

❑ *A Tested Plan for Being Successful in Your Classes*

❑ *Passing Tests Successfully*

❑ *Writing "A" Papers: How to Use the Library Well*

7

A Tested Plan for Being Successful in Your Classes

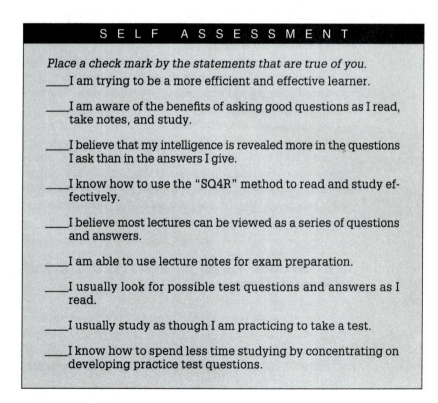

SELF ASSESSMENT

Place a check mark by the statements that are true of you.

____I am trying to be a more efficient and effective learner.

____I am aware of the benefits of asking good questions as I read, take notes, and study.

____I believe that my intelligence is revealed more in the questions I ask than in the answers I give.

____I know how to use the "SQ4R" method to read and study effectively.

____I believe most lectures can be viewed as a series of questions and answers.

____I am able to use lecture notes for exam preparation.

____I usually look for possible test questions and answers as I read.

____I usually study as though I am practicing to take a test.

____I know how to spend less time studying by concentrating on developing practice test questions.

The Key to Your Intelligence and Critical Thinking

What does being "intelligent" and "thinking critically" mean to you? Would you say that intelligent students who think critically have good vocabularies, are very knowledgeable, and solve problems easily? Are intelligent students and critical thinkers able to answer their instructors' questions and get high scores on tests? If one of your goals in life is to be an "intelligent" person and a "critical thinker," it's important for you to decide just what it is that you should know and be able to do!

Most college students believe they are intelligent people who think critically. A favorite pastime of many students and instructors in psychology and education is to discuss these topics: "What is intelligence? Is intelligence inborn? Can it be increased? Is an intelligent person creative? Street smart? Practical? Is there more than one kind of intelligence? If so, what different kinds are there? What is critical thinking?"

If you want to enhance your intelligence and critical thinking your best bet is to look for behaviors that are associated with intelligence and critical thinking. Most psychologists agree that an intelligent person who thinks critically is an efficient learner. He or she learns and remembers more than other people. But what behavior leads to this skill? The answer is *asking and answering questions.* An intelligent person who thinks critically asks important questions and searches for the answers.

Take vocabulary, for example. Many educators and psychologists believe that vocabulary is one of the best single indicators of intelligence. How does a person acquire a good vocabulary? By wondering, "What does that word mean?" and then finding the answer.

One way to find answers to vocabulary questions is to obtain a good, inexpensive dictionary and use it. Equally useful is asking what people mean when they use certain terms. Searching for the best words to describe something will improve your vocabulary and enhance your intelligence. Searching for information and answers to questions may be the key to improving your intelligence, enhancing your critical thinking skills, and helping you become more successful in school.

Asking Questions: The Key to Efficient Learning, Critical Thinking, and Success in Classes

If you talk with your friends or members of your success group about what a student must do to be successful, it will be clear to you that you must ask and answer good questions. You must do so when writing papers, reading your texts and notes, talking in discussion groups, attending classes, and taking tests.

Think of one of your textbooks. It consists of answers to many questions. Your instructors spend most of their time developing questions to ask you in class and on tests. Think of the notes you take. Are notes anything more than answers to questions? Your instructors have carefully analyzed important books, lectures, films, and other resources to generate a body of information that they present to you in class. The final task for you is to answer important questions about this information.

Let's look at simple and highly effective learning techniques developed at the University of Michigan. Students using these techniques report that once they learn to ask and answer intelligent questions, they become highly successful in school. They save hundreds of hours in studying and preparing for courses. As a result, they are able to spend more time going to movies, watching television, playing sports, being with friends, taking weekend trips, attending concerts, and leading the "good life."

If these things interest you, let's spend a little more time discussing how you can learn the correct strategies. One thing we promise is that you will achieve your academic goals with a great deal more pleasure and far less pain than you have known in the past. We sound one word of caution: Learning these new strategies may require you to change some of your old habits. Such changes are sometimes difficult or painful.

Why? Well, when you are used to a routine set of study habits, you often become comfortable with them and resist change. Even when you try the new study strategies and they seem to work, you'll have a tendency to go back to your old study habits. After all, these old habits have helped you accomplish your goals in the past. You have learned to live with them even though they may be time consuming and not as effective as you would like.

Once you become accustomed to the new study strategies, a lot of your old self-defeating habits and attitudes related to studying and becoming educated will fade away. You will begin to get some good feedback from professors, friends, and yourself that indicate that the new strategies save time. You will achieve your goals and have time to do things you never had time for in the past.

Principle I: Study to Pass Tests

Whenever you are reading out of curiosity, allow your mind to go in any direction it wishes. But, when you study, study as if you were practicing to take a test. Practice asking and answering questions. If you don't, you are wasting valuable time! After all, it's your time, so why waste it?

Doesn't studying as if you were practicing to take a test go against the idea of simply learning for the sake of learning?

When you focus your reading and studying by looking for answers to questions, you make the material meaningful and learn significantly more. Whether or not you are going to take a test on the material you are reading is secondary.

Your main aim is to develop the habit of getting the most out of your reading. To get the most out of your reading you need to focus on asking and looking for answers to questions.

Principle II: Ask Intelligent Questions

What is an intelligent question?

First, an intelligent question is a question you would like answered. *Second,* it is framed so that in seeking the answer you will learn new and useful information. *Third,* it might be close to a question your instructor asks on a test. *Fourth,* it can be a way to demonstrate what you already know.

How do you learn to ask intelligent questions?

Practice is the key to asking intelligent questions. Practice is a useful personal habit to acquire. At first it takes some work, but later questions arise out of habit.

What will good questions help you do?

Are you and your instructor interested in the same thing? You'll only know by asking questions. You may wish to study information which is of no interest to your instructor. That's fine. But regardless of your own interests, you want to make sure you do well in your course by knowing the information that your instructor defines as important.

If you ask good questions, you'll be able to focus on the important points of your lectures and readings. Good questions help you determine what your lecturers and the authors of your texts believe you should remember.

A major function of your questioning process should be to prepare you for exams. By practicing answering the questions you develop, you'll find out just how ready you really are to do well. After all, have you ever taken an exam that wasn't composed of questions your instructor wanted you to answer? That's why we cannot overemphasize the value of proving your brilliance by answering your questions!

Another point not to be overlooked is that you will please your instructors no end if you ask and answer good questions in class. The hundreds of hours you'll save in preparing to do well in your classes and on exams is clearly one of the hidden bonuses of the question-and-answer regimen we recommend.

What does a good question look like?

An intelligent question usually starts with a phrase such as:

Give several examples of...

Which of these is an example of ...

Describe the function of...

What is significant about...

List the important ...

Compare and contrast...

Interpret the following...

What is the structure of...

Identify the following...

Why does...

What does a completed good question look like?

A complete intelligent question might look like this:

Why do both your hunger pangs and your stomach contractions tend to decrease after lunch time even if you didn't eat anything?

How would you test your auditory threshold?

Compare the major psychological differences between chimpanzees and humans.

Give several examples of imperialism in South Africa during the early 1900s.

What functions are associated with the two hemispheres of the brain?

Principle III: Anticipate Your Instructor's Questions

. How can I predict what the instructor will think are important questions?

Pretend that you are the instructor and develop questions from your texts, lecture notes, and old exams. Think of questions before you go to class and then listen to find out whether or not other students ask the same questions or whether or not the instructor supplies answers to those questions.

Write out questions for a lecture or an assignment. Then ask your instructor whether or not he or she thinks these questions are important and what other questions you should attempt to answer.

Do not be afraid to ask your instructor what he or she thinks are the important questions. Most instructors are happy to tell you what they think is important. Give them a chance.

Ask your professor what goals he or she has for the students in the class. If you want a clear answer, you must learn to ask questions that help the professor clarify the questions he or she would like the class members to answer. You might ask:

> What should a student be able to do and what important questions should we be able to answer after having completed this chapter (unit, training, program)?

> What important questions do you think we should be looking at in this unit (chapter, assignment)?

> Can you suggest particular articles or books that highlight the issues we will be discussing in this unit?

> What important things should we be looking for in this particular reading (film, case study)?

When you ask questions like these, ask them in a positive manner. Students have a tendency to put instructors on the defensive. Think of it as your job to ask an instructor in what direction the course is headed and to reward him or her for telling you. A comment like "Thanks, that really clarifies things for me" is something most instructors appreciate.

Now that I know what intelligent questions are, what is the best way to get into the habit of developing questions and answers?

To help you become proficient at developing questions and answers, begin by focusing on your reading strategies. You can quickly learn how to get a lot more out of your reading by turning it into a question-answering process. We'll then discuss note taking, test taking, and a variety of other important study strategies. But because reading is the most important, that's where we'll begin.

Reading = Question Answering

Read to Find Questions and Answers

Studying your texts is not the same as reading your Sunday newspaper or other casual reading. Most textbooks are not written to entertain you. You can't get away with reading only the parts of texts that interest you. When it comes to studying, you want to choose reading strategies that motivate you to reach out mentally and emotionally and grasp important information.

Studying can be fun, but sometimes studying is very hard work, as hard as any physical labor. Your reading shouldn't seem like labor. But reading often seems like drudgery when you passively read your textbooks and lecture notes over and over without any focus. You need an active reading strategy that keeps you so focused that as you read the answers to your questions seem to bounce off the page at you.

The reading strategy we are suggesting will keep you awake, focused, and constantly aware of how much you are learning. When you use this strategy you will consistently find answers to important questions. Finding answers will excite you. Finding answers builds your confidence that you're learning what you want to learn and that you'll do well on your tests.

REMEMBER: The reading strategy you will learn is built on the premise that successful students view texts and notes as sources of questions and answers that are likely to appear on their exams. If you are not reading and studying textbooks and notes as if you are preparing to take a test, you are not using your time wisely.

Increase Your Reading Speed and Comprehension of Textbooks

One of the fastest ways to spend less time reading assignments is to learn how to figure out where the important information is located in your reading. You want to find the important questions and answers as quickly as possible.

It will help you to know that a large percentage (perhaps as many as 80 percent) of the words you read are not critical to your understanding of the important concepts. Most words simply link ideas. The *ideas* are the answers to the questions you wish to answer. So the strategy we are teaching you will show you how to determine where the important questions and answers are located. We don't want you wasting a lot of time focusing on information that isn't essential to grasping the important concepts.

Second, once you have found the important information, you need a strategy that helps you turn it into something meaningful that can be easily remembered. The strategy we will teach you focuses on turning information into answers. Why? Because when important information is restructured into answers, people remember it better. The key to comprehension and memory is restructuring information into meaningful answers. Go ahead and try this strategy to see how it improves the speed at which you read and your understanding of the material.

Reading Chapters in Textbooks

Survey-Question-Read-Recite-Write-Review: The SQ4R Strategy

Your comprehension of what you read will improve as you practice answering questions from your reading assignments. The strategy of reading to answer questions is considered by many experts on study skills and reading improvement to be the most efficient and effective means for getting the most out of your reading material in the least time.

To help you learn the SQ4R strategy, we recommend that you practice each step of the strategy on a textbook. Pick out a text for an introductory course such as psychology, biology, sociology, or anthropology. As you read through the following description of the SQ4R strategy, each time you come to an exercise, follow the directions to see how you can apply the SQ4R strategy to your text.

Step 1—Survey and Question

The goal of surveying a chapter is to determine two important pieces of information. What important questions are answered in the chapter? Where are the answers to the important questions located?

First, go to the beginning and end of the chapter to see whether or not there are chapter objectives, a list of questions, or a chapter summary. If so, read them right away! This is where you will find the important points that authors stress and the questions students should be able to answer after completing the chapter.

If you can answer the questions and already know what is in the summary, you probably won't have to read the chapter as thoroughly. But don't decide yet. If there is a set of questions, a list of objectives, or a chapter summary, you're ahead of the game; if not, you soon will be.

How do you survey? The process of surveying involves quickly skimming the chapter to determine what important questions it answers and where the answers are located. Look for titles, subtitles, illustrations, pictures, charts, lead sentences in paragraphs, and questions that will give you a basic idea of what the chapter is about.

While surveying, it is easy to turn titles, subtitles, and lead sentences into questions. For instance, "Alcoholism: Two Schools of Thought" is a paragraph heading in *Understanding Human Behavior*, a textbook written by McConnell and Philipchalk. You simply turn it into "What are two schools of thought about alcoholism?"

By writing questions as you survey, you keep yourself alert to the important points in the chapter. Reading becomes an active, goal-oriented process. As you survey, you formulate and write out questions that when answered, give you a good summary of the chapter. The result of your survey will be a list of questions and an idea of where the answers are located in the chapter.

To prove your brilliance, you may wish to try to answer the questions you developed while surveying before you even read the chapter. This self quiz tells you how much you already know about the chapter before spending an exorbitant amount of time reading. Many students are amazed at their ability to answer a large percentage of the questions they have formulated in their survey.

Another helpful strategy is to quickly summarize what you have learned about the chapter from your survey. By talking to yourself about the chapter, you help yourself focus on the important questions you should be able to answer after having read it.

Exercise for Step 1

Try surveying your own chapter. Your goal will be to develop 5–10 basic questions. You want to develop questions which, when answered, make you feel as though you have a good understanding of the basic concepts in the chapter. In addition to developing several important questions, your survey will give you a general feeling for where the answers to your questions are located.

As you survey your chapter, write down a few questions you believe cover the basic concepts presented in the chapter.

Here is space for you to write in the answers to your questions when you complete Step 3 of the SQ4R strategy.

1.

2.

3.

4.

5.

Step 2—Read to Answer Questions

It is now time to read your chapter. Read as quickly as you can. Read to find the answers to questions you developed while surveying the chapter and to find new questions and answers you didn't predict while surveying.

REMEMBER: In many instances, your questions and answers will be found in titles, subtitles, or the first few sentences of a paragraph. Occasionally, you will read well beyond the headings for more important details, but not with the regularity that caused you to waste time in the past reading over less important information.

Reading Selectively for Questions and Answers

When reading to answer questions, you read selectively. You read to find sources of information which answer your questions. When you come to a section of information which answers a question, you slow down and pay careful attention to the most important points which make up the answer to your question.

Reading this information is different than understanding it. To understand this information, you go through a process of working the information around in your mind, putting it into your own words until you have made up an answer which makes sense to you.

You then leave that information, start reading more rapidly, looking for the answer to your next question. When you find your next answer, you slow down, and start the process over again.

Reading at Different Rates

You can see that you are never reading at a constant rate. You read rapidly to find important information. When you come to the information, you spend time understanding it by turning it into an answer to a question, you then move on.

When you come to information that answers a question you hadn't predicted, you simply slow down, formulate the question, and make sure you know the answer. When you come to material with which you are very familiar, you don't spend a lot of time on it. You look it over quickly to see that there is nothing new. Then you keep going to find out what you don't know.

Reading to answer questions sounds reasonable. But how can I be sure I will remember the answer once I have read over the information?

When reading to answer questions, there is an important process that good readers follow. When you find information that answers a question, you need to restructure that information into an answer that makes sense to you. You need to make the information meaningful and easy to remember.

For example, when you see that a paragraph contains the answer to one of your questions, you don't try to memorize the paragraph. You read over the information in the paragraph and think through a meaningful answer.

As you read, you are always restructuring information so that it makes sense to you. Information is easiest to remember when it is restructured into answers. That is why as you watch good readers, you will see them looking over several paragraphs as they think and talk out an answer to a question.

Exercise for Step 2

Read through your chapter looking for answers to the questions you developed in Exercise 1. As you find your answers, stop and write them in the space provided in Exercise 1.

Step 3—Recite and Write Answers and Summaries

If you completed Exercises 1 and 2, you have accomplished the first three steps of SQ4R. You developed some questions, read to answer your questions, and talked and wrote out meaningful answers to your questions.

Reciting and writing the answers to your questions is the key to remembering the important information from your chapter. By restructuring the information into questions and answers, you'll improve your recall of the information. You can then use your questions and answers to help you prepare for your exams.

After you have recited and written your answers, you may want to try another strategy that will improve your recall of the chapter. Take a minute to summarize the chapter aloud. By talking to yourself about your answers and relating them to one another in a summary, you'll help improve your understanding of how all the concepts fit together.

Don't hesitate to talk to yourself (even if people think you're a little crazy) about the answers to your questions. Students often rush on to a new chapter before thoroughly proving to themselves that they are familiar with the information in the chapter they just read. They say to themselves, "I read it. I know what it's about." Don't make that mistake! Prove to yourself by answering your questions and summarizing your chapter that you really do comprehend the important information in your chapter.

Step 4—Review

If you have followed the steps so far, you are ready to review the chapter at any time. You will have a set of questions and answers representing the important information in the chapter. When preparing for your exam, you can quiz yourself on your questions until you know you can give accurate answers if the questions appear on your exam.

If you have practiced summarizing the chapter to yourself, you can compare your summary with the author's. Taken together, these activities will let you know that you've mastered the material. When you know you can answer questions correctly and make accurate summaries, you will be more confident that you understand the chapter and will do well on the exam.

The Result

You have now:

1. surveyed your chapter

2. developed questions

3. read selectively to answer your questions

4. found questions and answers that you hadn't predicted

5. recited and written meaningful answers to your questions

6 summarized the chapter silently or aloud

7. reviewed the chapter by answering your questions and summarizing the chapter.

If you followed these steps, you now have a basic understanding of the chapter.

This Book is an Example

For another example of how to use SQ4R, look at how this book is organized. "About This Book" explained the main objectives and purposes of *Student Success*. We listed questions students typically ask and then urged you to skim through the book rapidly to ask questions about it. Now you are reading the book in greater detail and talking about the new things you are learning (reciting) with yourself, your success group, or your study partners.

At the end of most chapters is an Action Review. The review questions help you specifically determine whether or not you are putting into practice what you are learning.

We wrote this book in a way that helps you put into practice what we know works for students!

Why should I believe that this approach works?

Evidence collected at the University of Michigan Reading and Learning Skills Center and other learning centers has shown that most good students use these strategies. When poor students learn SQ4R, they raise their grades, reduce study time significantly, increase reading speed, and improve comprehension of textbooks.

Advantages of SQ4R

SQ4R is designed to help you focus on learning what is important to you. You don't waste time reading and looking for things you already know. With SQ4R you spend less time memorizing facts that you will soon forget. You focus on learning as efficiently and effectively the important concepts in your texts and readings.

Your preparation for tests is a continual process. You learn to organize and structure your studying. You state your goals as questions, seek answers, achieve your goals, and move on. You focus on grasping the key concepts. Details are much easier to remember once you have grasped the big picture.

You learn to take an expert's point of view and to think things out for yourself. By the time you take the test, you will find that you have answered most of the important questions and feel confident that you have learned what is important to you.

Difficulties of SQ4R

It is difficult to change old study habits. You may be accustomed to reading every word, always afraid that you're going to miss something. A new strategy such as the SQ4R may appear reckless because you focus on learning what is important and not on trying to memorize everything you read.

It would be easy to stick with your old habits. It takes more energy to ask questions and develop summaries than it does to let your eyes passively read printed pages. It is easier just to open a book and start reading. With SQ4R, you study frequently for shorter periods of time, instead of waiting until the end of the course and cramming.

How can you reconcile advantages and disadvantages? There are advantages and disadvantages to everything! This is true for both successful and unsuccessful students. If there were no disadvantages, if it were easy, then everyone would be more successful. There are costs, but once you know SQ4R, the gains are worthwhile.

Imagine yourself agreeing to run in a 10-kilometer race several months from now. You will be running with friends, and it is important for all of you to do well. To be at your best, would you loaf around until the last few days and then prepare by running day and night until the time of the race? No. You'd start now with a weekly schedule of jogging and running. A little bit of practice on a regular basis is the best preparation. The same approach is true for effective studying and remembering.

Try the study techniques and look for results like the following:

> The quality of your questions and answers will improve with practice.

> The amount of time it takes you to develop questions, answers and summaries will decrease.

> The amount of time it takes to verify and improve your answers will decrease with practice.

> You will be able to cover large amounts of material in far less time.

> You will find that you are producing the same questions as your instructors, textbooks, and friends.

> With practice, you will find that the summaries you develop come closer to those of the author.

These techniques are based on several well-established principles of learning. When you learn information under conditions that are similar to those under which you will be tested, there is a greater likelihood that you will remember it. People learn information faster when it is meaningful and of some interest than when the information appears unrelated or confusing. Learning new material (answers) is easier when you associate it with familiar material (questions).

The SQ4R strategy sounds helpful, but could I start by just using parts of the strategy or using the whole strategy on small sections of my work?

Our students report best results when they begin practicing the entire strategy at once. But some people will adjust best to the SQ4R strategy by practicing on a small section of work in one course to see immediate results. They gradually increase the use of this method as they become more comfortable with it.

PREDICTING EXAM QUESTIONS

How do I go about predicting exam questions from sources other than my text?

Once you accept the value of always studying as if you were practicing to take a test, you'll be on the right track. It is important to gear your study behavior to collecting questions and answers that you expect to find on your exams. By using the reading strategies we have suggested, you will have a good start. Your reading will always be geared to asking and answering important questions.

In addition to this style of reading, there are several other strategies that will help you to collect a good set of exam questions. Taking notes, asking friends and instructors, collecting old exams, holding discussion groups, and using textbook and study guide questions are several we suggest. Let's start with taking notes in class.

Sources of Exam Questions

Active Learning

Attend Class

Attending class is such an obviously useful thing to do that we're almost embarrassed to have to mention it. Yet, in a research study reported by H.C. Lindgren, it was found that there is an important relationship between attending class and grades received. A comparison of grade point averages and class attendance showed these percentages:

Grade Point Average vs Class Percentages

Class Attendance	% of Students with B Average or Higher	% of Students with C- Average or Lower
Always or almost always present	85	48
Sometimes absent	8	7
Often absent	7	45

The percentages in the table suggest that attending class always or almost always helps maximize your chances of success. The percentages indicate that the student who is often absent will probably receive low grades.

Utilize the First Lecture

Successful students are active in determining the requirements for each course. During the first class sessions, they typically find out answers to the following key questions. Place a check in front of the questions you typically ask during the first few days of class:

_____ Which chapters in the textbook will be covered?

_____ When will the exams be given?

_____ What material will each exam cover?

_____ What type of questions will be on the exams—essay, multiple choice?

_____ What other work will be required?

_____ When will the work be due?

_____ How will the work be evaluated?

_____ How will grading in the course be determined?

_____ Does the instructor have an outline of the most important terms and concepts to be covered?

_____ Should textbook chapters be read before lectures?

_____ What does the instructor hope each student will understand by the end of the course?

These questions are a starting point. Others will occur as you go along.

REMEMBER: Be cautious about making instructors feel they are being cross-examined. Be assertive, but *tactful.* If an instructor is not prepared to answer all these questions, back off. Try to find out when the information may be available. In general, you will find that instructors enjoy answering questions about what they believe is most valuable in their courses. A few instructors may be poorly prepared, however, and could become defensive if pressed too hard.

Some instructors will have the answers to most of these questions on written handouts. If you don't receive a handout, be sure to write everything down in your notebook.

Take Lecture Notes

By writing down what the instructor says in lectures, you are helping yourself become an active listener. You are also being realistic about the nature of human memory. Human beings quickly forget most of what they hear, no matter how much they would like to be able to remember.

Several days after hearing a lecture, most students can at best recall about 10 percent of what was said. So, unless you tape-record the lectures or alternate note taking with a friend, you need to take notes at every lecture.

Some students don't take notes. They may be trying to experiment to see whether or not they can get by without note taking. These students may have reasons for wanting everyone to know that they are not involved in the course. They may be trying to impress you with how smart they are. At any rate, if you ask a student who doesn't take notes to fill you in on something the instructor said last week, you will quickly learn for yourself how important note taking is for accurate remembering.

Use Lecture Notes as a Source of Exam Questions and Answers

You'll put yourself at a tremendous advantage if you can accustom yourself to think of your instructor's lectures as sessions that provide answers to important questions. When you actively use your notes to quiz yourself on important questions that are likely to appear on your exams, you'll walk into your exams feeling confident and well-prepared.

REMEMBER: Use your notes to learn more and do better on your exams. If you remember the formula, *notes = exam questions and answers*, you'll learn more, do well on your exams, and live happily ever after.

Lecture Notes

Think of your lectures as textbook chapters. Just like a chapter, each lecture usually has a main theme and makes several important points. If you listen for the main points of each lecture, they will be easier to hear.

During lectures, most instructors answer several questions rather thoroughly. If your instructor only alludes to an answer, you'll have to go to outside sources to get the information you need.

Your job during the lecture is to record the most important information given. Don't restrict your note taking to only those statements made by the instructor. Be alert to classroom discussions in which students are asked questions by the instructor. After the lecture, use study time to develop questions that are answered by information in your notes.

Tips on Taking Notes

Keep a notebook for each course. Write your name, address, and phone number in each notebook. Use large pages for taking notes. Put the notes from each class session on separate pages. Put the date on each day's class notes.

Use an outline form whenever possible.The most commonly used outline form is this:

    I. (Roman numerals for major topics)
    A. (Capital letters for major subgroups)
        1. (Numbers for supporting examples, people,
            points)
        2.
    B.
        1.
            a.(small letters for supporting details)
            b.
            c.
        2.
        3.

We encourage you to take lecture notes in an outline form. This habit will help you focus on listening for and recording main points that you can turn into questions and answers. The outline form helps create an orderliness to information that might otherwise appear confusing. Our chief concern is that you record all the information you need to develop good questions and answers. The following hints will help ensure that you listen for and record the main points of every lecture.

Example: Layout for note taking

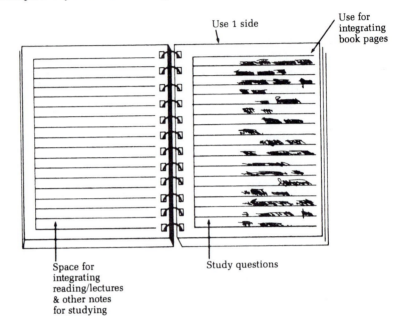

Use 1 side

Use for integrating book pages

Space for integrating reading/lectures & other notes for studying

Study questions

Steps for Taking Notes

1. Take notes in a spiral notebook, using a separate notebook for each course. Write your lecture notes on the right-hand page. Leave a wide margin on the left for writing in probable test questions. Leave the left-hand page blank. Later you will use the back of each preceding left-hand page to integrate reading, lecture, and other notes while you are studying.

   NOTE: There is an important point you want to consider about integrating your lecture and reading notes. You will often find yourself reading a book that presents information relevant to a topic covered in your lecture notes. You may say to yourself, "I ought to combine some of this information from the book with my lecture notes." The problem is that you don't really want to stop reading to do this. There is a simple solution. You just need to follow one procedure.

   Write the page number from the book you're reading which covers the important material, on the right-hand margin of the page in your lecture notes where similar information is covered. Later on when you review your notes, you can flip open the text to the page you have noted. You can then integrate important information from your text with your notes.

2. Write down the major ideas and statements in the lecture. Don't try to write down every word, just key phrases and ideas. Underline points that your instructor emphasizes.

3. After the lecture, fill in missing ideas and key words and phrases. Underline headings that are of major significance. You may also wish to compare your notes with a friend's to see what you may have missed.

4. After each lecture, take several minutes to turn your notes into questions, focusing on the main theme and subtopics. Each lecture will usually supply three to seven good exam questions. The questions should be written in the left-hand margin.

5. At least once a week, review the questions you have asked. Pretend you are taking a test. Give yourself an oral quiz, or even better, practice by taking a written quiz. Then compare your answers with those given in your notes or textbook.

REMEMBER: This procedure will help you make something meaningful out of lectures that often leave you in a quandary. Your purpose is to go to lectures looking for questions and their answers. If you leave each lecture with several questions and answers, you should be pleased. They're likely to be on your next test!

See the example of notes taken at an introductory psychology lecture. The topic was operant conditioning.

Application

Follow Steps 1 through 4 for taking lecture notes in your next class. Discover how complete and efficient your learning can be while you are also becoming quickly ready for tests. Show several classmates what you are doing and tell them what it feels like to use this method.

Old Exams

Students are often made to feel guilty when they admit to having looked over past exams. The implication is that if you have looked over old exams, you have been cheating. Our answer to this is, bunk! Old exams tell you what an instructor thinks is important information for which you should be responsible.

Looking at old exams doesn't guarantee that you'll know exactly what your exam questions will be. Instructors change their lectures, textbooks, films, guest speakers, and even their opinions once in a while. Consequently, exams change from semester to semester.

AN EXAMPLE OF NOTE TAKING

Intro Psych—Oct. 26, I. Topic: Operant Conditioning

Questions	Notes
	A. B.F. Skinner conducted pioneering research
	1. worked with rats and pigeons
	2. designed special cages– "Skinner boxes"
What is an important belief of B.F. Skinner?	3. believes "Behavior is determined by its consequences"
What is another term for operant conditioning?	B. Basis for operant conditioning (also called instrumental learning)
Why do psychologists use the term "reinforcement" instead of "reward"?	1. a voluntary behavior is followed by a reinforcer—not called a reward because some rewards do not act as reinforcers
	2. reinforcement increases the probability that a behavior will be repeated
	3. reinforcement variables:
	a. amount
	b. schedule
	1. 100%-continuous
	2. fixed-ratio and fixed-interval
	3. variable-ratio and variable-interval
Will punishment usually eliminate behavior?	4. punishment can temporarily suppress behavior but seldom eliminates it
What is spontaneous recovery?	5. negative reinforcement-behavior increases when unpleasant stimulus removed
	6. extinction of behavior
	a. from withdrawal of reinforcer
	b. after time lapse reappearance called spontaneous recovery

Questions	**Notes**

What are the main elements of a behavior modification program?	C. Application of principles
	  1. Behavior modification program
	    a. terminal response or goal stated, must be observable and measurable
	    b. current level of desired behavior observed—called baseline
	    c. any baseline behavior directed toward the terminal goal is reinforced: all other behaviors ignored

What terms are used to describe the method of reinforcing any small step in the right direction?	d. each small step is reinforced—is called:
	      1. shaping
	      2. method of successive approximations
	      3. tracking positives
	  2. Uses with humans—contingency management
	    a. programs for brain-damaged children
	    b. improve academic performance
	    c. programs for psychiatric patients
	    d. improve performance in business

Nevertheless, by looking at old exams you may answer several important questions:

1. Does the instructor have some favorite questions that he or she asks every year?
2. Do test questions appear to be taken from material similar to that which you are studying?
3. Do test questions come primarily from lecture notes or from a variety of sources?
4. What types of questions does the instructor prefer? Multiple choice, short answer, true-false, essay?
5. On which content areas does the instructor place the most emphasis?

These questions should help you see the value of reading and taking notes in the question-answer format. There is no guarantee that the instructor will take most of the questions from the same source that he or she used in years past. Yet it is surprising how similar questions are from year to year regardless of the textbooks that instructors use. They often chose new textbooks that give better answers to the same questions they have been asking for many years.

Equally important, few instructors make drastic changes in their course notes from semester to semester. Instructors usually update notes. The questions you develop from course notes, textbooks, and other sources, combined with old exam questions, will be invaluable in your exam preparation.

Textbooks

You put yourself at a great advantage when you read the questions that precede or follow the chapter. Such questions are included by authors because they believe that students should be able to answer them after having read the chapter.

Many instructors take their test questions directly from questions in the textbook. Surprisingly, many students never look at these questions. They seem to feel that no instructor could be so stupid as to use questions similar to those found in the chapter.

Authors usually try to help students, not trick them! If you are not in the habit of answering chapter questions, we recommend you use them as the starting point in your effort to organize a good set of questions and answers.

Student Study Guides

Student study guides that accompany many of your texts are excellent sources of exam questions. Study guides are designed to show you what students using the textbook should know. Study guides often contain true-false, multiple-choice, fill-in, short essay questions, and other exercises. Even if your exam is likely to be made up of questions that differ in style from questions found in the study guide, the questions in the guide are still extremely valuable.

You only have to relate the answers to the guide's questions to those likely to be found on your next exam. Study guides are designed to teach you important concepts and save you time. The time you save can be used for other important activities, like watching television or taking a nap.

NOTE: *The publisher of your textbook may have a study guide available even if your instructor does not require its use.* Check this out—especially for introductory textbooks. Ask your instructor. If a study guide exists, you can purchase it through the bookstore or directly from the publisher. Sales figures from textbook publishers show that 7 out of 10 students using textbooks do *not* purchase and use the accompanying study guides. Yet, research has shown that students who use study guides tend to learn more and earn better grades than students who don't.

Discussion Groups and Friends

Some of your best sources of test questions, yet often the most overlooked, are friends and fellow students. By talking with other students enrolled in the course or with students who have been enrolled in past semesters, you can judge the types of questions and answers you should be looking for. At the same time, these students can tell you where you should spend less time.

Many students believe it's difficult to organize formal study groups. Some students simply prefer to work on their own. This strategy can be self-defeating. By organizing the questions and answers from a variety of sources, you are in an excellent position to compare yours with those of fellow students.

Compare this process to the pastime of trading cards, in which you collect as many cards as you can and simply trade off your extras to build up an even stronger set. Similarly, you find out what questions other students feel are important. You compare your answers to theirs to ensure that you haven't overlooked important information. Everyone comes out stronger. Everyone is better prepared to ask and answer intelligent questions.

By studying in a group or with one other person, you will help to ensure that you benefit in some important ways. Which of the following do you think would be a benefit to you of working with other people?

___ I would structure a situation in which other people encouraged me to develop study habits recommended in *Student Success*.

___ I would ask and answer more questions that are important and likely to be found on my exams.

___ I would learn of questions I hadn't predicted.

___ I would refine my answers with additional information supplied by other students.

___ I would put together more practice tests.

___ I would take more practice tests.

___ I would develop a more efficient and effective process of preparing for exams.

Instructors

Your instructor is the best source of information on forthcoming tests. Many students find it difficult to ask instructors what they believe is important. As we suggested earlier, most instructors are happy to tell you what they think is important. Give them a chance: Ask them!

Ask your instructor: "Could you make some suggestions about the areas in which we should concentrate our studying?" "Are there particular topics that you feel we should devote more time to than others?"

Whatever you do, *don't* ask: "Are there any areas you feel are unimportant?" "Which of these chapters should we spend less time on, considering all that we have to study for this test?" If you ask such questions, the instructors may be so peeved they will assign the encyclopedia. Most instructors believe that everything they teach is important.

In trying to determine what is likely to be on exams, your goal is simply to encourage your instructors to narrow down all the important things they have told you to a precise statement of what your exam will look like. If you are pleasant and thank your instructors for their help, you'll be ahead of the game. You may even find out the exact form of the exam and which questions are most important.

The Result

Predicting exam questions is the most useful technique we have found in preparing students to learn the important concepts covered in their courses. Equally important, it helps students do well on their exams with much greater ease. If you have followed our suggestions, you will have collected exam questions from:

1. your textbook chapters
2. lists of chapter objectives
3. your lecture notes
4. old exams
5. lists of questions in your textbooks
6. lists of questions in student study guides
7. discussion groups and friends
8. your instructors

Once you have collected a good set of test questions, you will be better prepared to follow through with the strategies we suggest in the next section on tests.

Is the purpose of education to learn how to answer instructors' questions and do well on tests?

The conflict between learning what one is curious about versus learning to do well on tests is an old dilemma. Fortunately it is not an either/or choice. In most cases there are ways to accommodate the interests of both the learner and the instructor.

If you want to understand the experts and even go beyond them, it is important to be able to ask and answer the same questions that experts believe are important. If you're realistic, you know you have to pass the requirements of the course. If you understand what your instructor wants, you will learn a lot. If your instructor is less than adequate, it is a matter of meeting his or her criteria and going on to better courses. There is no need to waste time in the process.

How can developing questions for class help me if I'm afraid of being called on in class?

When you prepare questions and answers and practice, you will be less afraid. It is natural to be afraid if you are not prepared. Talk to yourself about the answers to questions your instructors are likely to ask in class. Once you have proven to yourself that you know the answers, you will be less fearful about your ability to answer similar questions in class. Language labs and discussion groups are useful places to begin to practice answering questions your instructors might ask in class.

If the fear comes from a general fear of having everyone look at you when you talk, find out what is available on campus in the way of professional counseling, assertiveness workshops, or classes in verbal communications. If you ask around, you will find that there are usually some professional counselors or faculty members who are very good at helping shy people become more comfortable speaking in groups.

❏ ACTION REVIEW: Develop a Checklist for Successful Studying

Here is a list of guidelines that will help you to monitor your studying and your success at using the learning strategies we've described. Consider placing this list in a visible location where it can constantly remind you of the study habits that will lead to Student Success.

____ I am using the SQ4R strategy out of habit for learning course material.

____ I survey my reading first, ask questions, and then read to answer questions.

____ I practice writing answers to questions and developing chapter summaries.

____ I develop questions and answers from lectures, textbooks, chapter objectives and summaries, study guides, old tests, discussion groups, and friends.

____ I ask my instructors questions that assist me to determine how I should study for their courses.

____ I keep a weekly record of the number of questions and answers I develop for each class?

____ I reward myself for developing questions and answers.

❏ ACTION GUIDELINES: Start Developing Questions and Answers

There is no better time to begin developing and answering exam questions! You will find it useful to count questions and answers you collect from textbooks, old exams, lecture notes, study guides, discussion groups, classmates, and your instructors.

Create a chart that you can put in a highly visible location, if possible, in your regular study area. As you develop your questions and answers for each class, record your progress on your chart. Set some goals for the number of questions you want to develop in each course and reward yourself regularly when you achieve your goals. Show your success group partners what you are accomplishing. Talk about how it feels to use this study method.

❏ ACTION GUIDELINES: Form a Study Group

Ask several friends who are taking the same course to meet right after class or at a convenient time. Using your notes, review what was discussed in the lecture to determine what questions may appear on the test.

From any lecture there are unlikely to be more than five to seven major questions that could appear on a test. Divide the questions up and have everyone write answers to his or her questions. Each member of the group will use whatever sources of information are necessary to develop what he or she thinks would be a complete answer to the question, were it to appear on the exam.

At your next meeting, each person will distribute copies of the answers to their questions. In addition, each person will take on several new questions from the most recent lecture.

It is important for the group to establish criteria for a good answer. Answers should not take hours to produce. Develop an answer that is complete and could be easily reproduced during the time allotted on the exam. Some students feel pressured to produce too much to ensure that the other members of the group will be impressed. Don't get caught in that bind. This activity is designed to teach you how to work as a team, to share responsibility, learn from one another what goes into a good answer, and help each person save time.

SUCCESS GROUP ACTIVITIES

1.   Talk with each other about how well the SQ4R method is working for each of you. What difficulties are there in making it work? What successes have you had? What can you do to encourage and support each other's efforts to master this study strategy? Does it help to modify or rename any of the steps? Is it more appealing, for example, to call step one "scan" instead of "survey"?

  2.   Discuss the dilemma many students have at some time during college: Do you learn for learning's sake and the enjoyment of acquiring knowledge or for the sake of passing the instructor's tests? What are your thoughts and feelings about this question? Is it a big problem? A minor one? Do you care?

8

Passing Tests Successfully

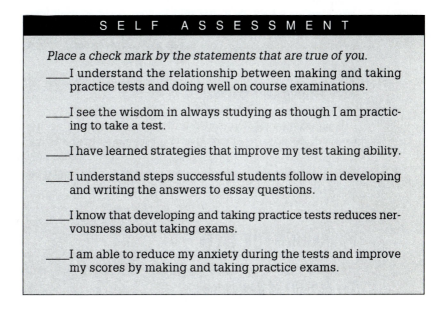

S E L F A S S E S S M E N T

Place a check mark by the statements that are true of you.

____I understand the relationship between making and taking practice tests and doing well on course examinations.

____I see the wisdom in always studying as though I am practicing to take a test.

____I have learned strategies that improve my test taking ability.

____I understand steps successful students follow in developing and writing the answers to essay questions.

____I know that developing and taking practice tests reduces nervousness about taking exams.

____I am able to reduce my anxiety during the tests and improve my scores by making and taking practice exams.

GUARANTEE YOUR SUCCESS ON TESTS

Have you ever taken an exam that didn't require you to answer questions? Probably not. Exams in music, physical education, art, and other classes in which you perform are exceptions of course. In most cases, however, your grades are determined by your answers to questions.

Your learning and success in college are dependent upon an important skill. You have to be able to answer questions posed by your instructors in class and on exams. That is why every time you read your course notes or texts, you should be looking for potential exam questions.

> **IF YOU WANT TO LEARN ALL YOU CAN AND DO WELL ON TESTS, ALWAYS STUDY AS THOUGH YOU'RE PRACTICING TO TAKE A TEST.**

It makes sense that if you want to do well on your exams, you practice taking exams. You'll use the strategies described in Chapter 7 to develop exam questions from notes, texts, and other sources. You'll then use the strategies in this chapter to prepare for and take tests.

The fact is that most students don't prepare for exams by taking practice tests. Most students prepare for exams by reading and re-reading their notes, texts, and other sources of information. Have you ever known instructors who asked you to come to an exam and read your notes or textbook to them? Absolutely not! Your instructors ask you to answer questions developed from their lecture notes, your texts, and other sources.

Your Strategy for Success

You want to develop the habit of making up exams just like the ones you believe your instructors will give you. Get your friends to quiz you on exams they have developed. Above all, develop a realistic means of learning to pass exams. Just as orchestras rehearse for concerts and football teams play practice games, prepare for exams by taking exams.

PREPARING FOR TESTS

The Benefits of Reviewing

Now that I have collected a good set of questions and answers, how can I make sure that I'll do well on the tests?

Periodically, review the questions you have developed to see whether or not you can still answer them. Avoid saying to yourself, "I know the answer to that one." Prove to yourself how brilliant you have become: *Orally and in writing, practice answering your questions.*

The habit of reviewing is easy to develop. You sit down between and after classes and talk out, think out, or write out answers to questions. Rather than sitting around wondering whether you are doing well in your courses, you prove to yourself that you can answer the future test questions.

A Test Preparation Strategy

Periodically reviewing your questions and answers is a great habit to develop. The habit of actually taking practice tests is equally beneficial.

The strategy focuses on several principles. Check which of these principles you regularly follow.

_____ Using the questions I have collected, I make up practice tests.

_____ I take practice tests under conditions as close as possible to the actual conditions in which I'll be tested.

_____ After I test myself, I compare my answers with the answers I developed from my textbooks, lecture notes, and other sources.

Quiz Yourself

Here are some specific hints about making and taking practice tests, strategies for taking tests, and other useful exam preparation strategies.

Using Your Notes

When you quiz yourself from the questions and answers in your notebook, cover up your answers with a blank sheet of paper. After answering each question orally or in writing, remove the paper and check to see how accurately you have answered your question.

This system allows you to quiz yourself quickly by looking at your questions, providing written or oral answers, and then checking to see how well your quiz answers compare with your original answers.

Most students like this system because it gives them a central filing system of questions and answers. Rather than fumbling through lecture notes and textbooks, they go to their notebooks of questions and answers.

Answering Math and Science Questions

What you have said about developing questions and answers sounds great for most students, but what about those of us who spend most of our time working problems in math and science? How can this technique help us?

One of the most important insights you can develop is the recognition that success in a particular course is based upon solving specific problems, especially in mathematics, chemistry, physics, and other courses with a heavy emphasis on computational and problem-solving skills.

Your reviews for math and science courses should be no different from those for other courses. To be successful, you need to practice working problems as similar as possible to those that will be found on your next exam. By working sample problems in your notebook or on 4 by 6 inch cards, you will develop files of important problems you should be able to solve on your test.

When you prepare for tests which require problem solving, you want to do exactly that, practice solving problems. It will be especially helpful for you to work with other students in the course. You want to find out what types of problems they believe will be on your exam. Equally important, you want to see the steps they follow when solving the problems.

Preparing for Language Exams

How about students of foreign languages? Should they review in the same way?

If you are taking a foreign language, you have a very discrete set of skills to master. Your strategy for being successful as much as ever focuses on preparing for tests by practicing answering important questions that are likely to appear on your next exam.

Language students must maintain basic vocabulary and grammatical skills if they wish to develop more complex language skills. By reviewing these areas, language students assure themselves of continued involvement in the basics upon which more complex skills are built.

Your language courses will require you to quiz yourself on a daily basis over the vocabulary and structure of the language you are learning. Your language labs offer you an opportunity to practice developing your language skills. Every exercise you complete, whether from your text, a workbook, or on tape will require that you answer a question or demonstrate that you have mastered vocabulary or new language skills.

MAKING AND TAKING PRACTICE TESTS

Making and taking practice tests will benefit you in many ways. One important benefit is that you practice exactly what is required of you in the testing situation, asking and answering intelligent questions. In addition, your practice tests will help you relax and build your confidence. After successfully passing practice tests, you are less likely to feel tense and uneasy. You should sleep much better knowing you have studied good questions and answers.

The Steps for Practice Tests

1. You first estimate the amount of time you'll be given to take your instructor's exam. You then take your practice test over the same length of time. Taking your tests under realistic time pressure is important. Once you see that you can answer a reasonable number of questions in whatever time is allotted, you'll feel more comfortable when you're in the actual testing situation.

2. Arrange the questions you've been accumulating from chapters, lecture notes, study groups, old exams, and other sources into practice tests.

3. If possible, test yourself on questions that are in the same format that your instructor's test will offer (multiple choice, short essay, and so on). This is where old tests come in handy. By practicing on old tests, you'll be more likely to be comfortable with your instructor's test. Study guides are also useful because guides contain many questions in a variety of formats.

    If all the questions you have developed from your notes and texts are short-answer questions and your test is going to be composed of multiple-choice questions, you needn't rewrite your questions to fit into a multiple-choice format. By quizzing yourself on your questions, you will be learning the information necessary to do well on your instructor's test, regardless of the format.

4. Take your practice tests under conditions as similar as possible to those under which you'll be tested. The classroom in which you'll be tested is the best place to take practice tests. If it is not available to you, make sure you practice in a room where you won't be bothered.

5. Try to answer your questions without referring to your books or other sources of information.

6. When attempting to answer questions for which you need more information, try to use whatever information you have to formulate a reasonable answer. Pretend you are in a real test and are trying to earn at least partial credit. This strategy forces you to take what you already know and to determine what might be the answer rather than saying, "I just don't know!"

    There are really very few situations in which you "Just don't know!" Writing out an answer that makes sense to you, even though you don't remember exactly what was said in the textbook or lecture is a reasonable approach. You often know more than you think. An imaginative answer may not answer the question you were asked, but your instructor may give you some points for trying to "think the question out."

7. Once you have completed the test, compare your answers with those you have in your own set of questions and answers.

8. After noting the questions you have answered well and those in need of improvement, design a new test. Follow the same procedure that we have outlined in Steps 1–7. Take the new test and continue repeating the steps until you think you have mastered all the questions and answers likely to appear on your instructor's test.

Weekly and Final Practice Tests

When you take weekly practice tests in each subject, you'll find that exam panic, last-minute cramming, and test anxiety tend to be a thing of the past. It may sound like a lot of work to develop a weekly test or quiz for each course you are taking, but can you think of a better method of testing to see how well you are learning?

Before each scheduled test, take a comprehensive practice test made up of sample questions from your weekly tests. You'll be pleasantly surprised at how much easier it is to pass your final practice test when you have been taking weekly tests.

Taking weekly tests allows you to master small amounts of information each week and then to put everything together in a final practice test just before you take the real thing.

Advantages of Preparing for Tests by Taking Tests

But isn't this strategy very time consuming?

It may appear so, but students who collect test questions and answers, take weekly practice tests (or quizzes), and take final practice tests spend far less time on irrelevant and wasteful studying. These students practice exactly what their instructors will require of them, "asking and answering intelligent questions."

Such students also obtain a more solid education. They remember what they have learned much better than students who cram for exams. Research into forgetting, done originally by Ebbinghaus and replicated many times over, shows that people quickly forget most of what they learn unless they review and rehearse the material.

We have assumed in our suggested study strategies that you want to pass tests well and obtain an excellent education. Your success in life after college is a function of what you can do, not of your grades. When you go to an attorney to have a contract drawn up, do you ask, "What grade did you receive in contract law?" Or if you have a pulled muscle, do you ask the physician about his or her scores on anatomy tests? No. You seek help or services on the basis of what people know and can do.

To obtain learning that lasts, each of us must apply the basic principles of learning. Otherwise, we end up with average grades but little knowledge.

Does making and taking practice tests reduce test anxiety?

As noted, exam panic and last-minute cramming are unlikely to occur if you follow our suggestions for studying and exam preparation. What makes most people anxious is that they practice study behaviors and thought processes that are not similar to what is going to be required of them in the test. If people don't practice what is going to be expected of them, it makes sense that they will be anxious, especially when they walk into the test and see that everything they studied only faintly resembles what is being asked.

For example, if you are going to be asked to work chemistry problems on an exam, you have to practice working problems as you prepare. If your English instructor is going to ask you to answer five short-answer essay questions about modern authors, you have to practice writing answers to short-answer essay questions.

If you try to predict test questions and practice answering your questions, it is unlikely you will walk into an exam and find questions that are totally different from those you predicted. The minute you see that your instructor's questions resemble your own, your anxiety will decrease. The more you practice developing good test questions and practice taking tests, the faster you will see your test anxiety drop to a reasonable level.

TAKING YOUR INSTRUCTOR'S TESTS

Now that you know how to prepare for a test, let's make sure that you know how to relax and use your time wisely once you have the real test in your hands. These rules apply to all forms of exams whether they be essay or multiple-choice.

General Rules

Survey Your Test

Read the instructions to determine the types of questions you'll be expected to answer.

Skim through the test to determine what it looks like and where you'll earn the most points.

Don't spend too much time reading questions.

Quickly form a basic idea of how the test is set up and plan your attack.

Plan How to Spend Your Time

Divide your time to ensure that you schedule enough for all portions of the test. Otherwise, you'll devote too much time to the most difficult parts and will "choke" when you find that you won't be able to complete the whole test.

Figure Out Where and How You Get the Most Points

Before starting, determine whether or not answering the easier questions will earn you as many points as answering the more difficult questions. If so, complete the easy questions first. After answering them you'll have more confidence, and you will be able to go on to the more difficult questions.

Figure Out What the Question Is Asking For

Make sure you understand what each question is asking. If the directions say, "Give several examples of . . . ," do exactly that. Give instructors exactly what they ask for. Don't twist questions into something else.

Don't Get Stuck on Difficult Questions

If you don't understand a question or find it extremely difficult, place an "X" by it and move on to easier questions. You can come back later. This procedure saves time and prevents anxiety. Most important, you may find the answer hidden in other questions as you move through the test. Don't waste precious time trying to dig out the answers from the back of your brain. Expect the answer to come to you as you work on other items, just as you do when trying to recall a person's name. Relaxing and expecting the name to come to you in a few moments works better than struggling to remember.

Leave Time to Review Your Work

Be sure to leave yourself a few minutes at the end of the exam to go over each section to see that you haven't forgotten to answer any questions.

TWO KINDS OF EXAMINATIONS: RECOGNITION AND RECALL

Most of your exams in college will be one of two different kinds. One requires you to *recognize* the correct answer to a question. The other requires you to *recall* from memory the answer to a question.

Tests of Recognition

There are three kinds of tests that require you to recognize the correct answer to a question: multiple-choice, true-false, and matching. The most popular is multiple-choice. It requires you to identify the correct answer among four or five choices listed.

Next most popular are true-false tests that ask you to indicate if a statement is correct or not. Instructors don't use true-false items very much because you have a 50-percent chance of getting the answer right through dumb luck.

Another recognition test, less frequently used, is called matching. It requires you to match or pair off the items on one list with items on a second list. Each type of recognition test requires a different test-taking strategy.

Multiple-Choice Questions

Never leave an answer blank unless there is a penalty for guessing. Read questions carefully but answer them quickly. If the answer is not immediately obvious to you, check off a tentative answer and come back to it. Later items in the test often give clues to the answers in earlier items.

As you answer multiple-choice questions, always be sure to eliminate the obviously incorrect answers first. You will save considerable time and will help to reduce anxiety about choosing the correct answer.

If after reading the question and all options the answer isn't immediately apparent, wait a second before you look at the options again. First, look at the question and try to develop an answer. Then look at the options to see if the answer isn't more apparent. Many students report that this is a useful technique.

If a multiple-choice question doesn't make sense, read the question and each of the answers independently. By combining the question and the answers one at a time, you may figure out what the question is asking.

If the question is quite clear but none of the options seems to make sense, try combining the question with each option one at a time. Reading all four options together may create confusion. But by combining them independently with the question, one may stand out as correct.

When an "all of the above" option is available, be careful. Only when you can't eliminate one option will "all of the above" be correct. The same warning holds true for "none of the above." Unless you can find an obvious flaw in each answer, "none of the above" is not your answer.

Read the Instructions Carefully

Be sure the instructor wants only one correct answer for each multiple-choice question. Few instructors develop multiple-choice questions with more than one correct answer. Be sure that your instructor isn't the exception.

Consider all options. Don't select the first one that looks good and forget to read the others. Sometimes instructors place a good, but not the best, option first to catch students who don't read each answer carefully. Read all options to make sure that you have chosen the best.

Be cautious when an answer includes such absolute words as *every, always, and never.* There are few situations in which something is always or never true.

Read and answer each question quickly. Look for key words and phrases such as "Which is *not* . . ." or "*According to* Skinner . . ." or "The *strongest* evidence . . ." After you have answered all questions, go back to see that you have read them correctly. If you have time, reread them all. If not, reread those that you marked with "X" the first time through because you were unsure of your answers.

Contrary to the popular advice about never changing answers, it can be to your advantage to change answers. The research evidence shows that when students have prepared well for an examination, the number of students who gain by changing answers is significantly greater than the number of students who lose by changing answers. Be cautious about changing answers, of course. But your second thought, if you have prepared well, may be more correct than following a widely held belief that is not supported by research evidence.

True-False Questions

Don't waste time pondering true-false questions. Some students waste major portions of test periods on true-false questions. If you don't know the answer right away, don't become frustrated. Simply move on to the next question. One or two questions aren't worth that many points. They don't deserve the precious time that could be devoted to other, more important questions. Besides, the answers you don't recall on a true-false question may be remembered on another part of the examination.

Matching Questions

Check to make sure you have read the directions for matching questions carefully. Sometimes students believe that matches are so obvious that they do exactly the opposite of what is asked. If the instructions say, "Match those that are different" or "Match those that are opposite," you'll feel rather foolish if you have spent a lot of time matching those that are similar.

It saves time to answer the easy questions first. This tactic reduces the chance of guessing incorrectly on more difficult matches.

Tests of Recall

Written examinations require you to recall the answer to a question from memory. Tests of recall are more difficult than tests of recognition. Written tests of recall include writing long essays, writing short answers to questions, or filling in the missing words in a sentence. A long essay examination may ask you to answer only one question or at the most two, three, or four, depending on how much time you are given for the exam. Long essay examinations ask you to "Trace the development of . . ." or "Explain and provide supporting evidence for each of the theoretical views . . ."

A short-answer essay exam has more questions. On it you might be asked to "Briefly compare and contrast . . ." or "What are the major characteristics of . . ."

To do well on any written answer test you must pay careful attention to the key instruction in the question. The most common instruction terms are: define, compare, list, contrast, analyze, explain, outline, summarize, name, and describe.

Short-Answer Essay Questions

Short-answer essay questions will ask you to:

define each of the terms and concepts in a list

outline an experiment or study

list the main points in favor of a theory

give three criticisms against a theory or report of a study

draw and correctly label a chart, graph, or structure
(for example, a nerve cell)

name the basic steps or stages in a process.

The answers to short-answer essay questions will be short sentences, incomplete sentences, or lists that show you understand the main points. Be sure to emphasize definitions of terms and concepts. Your aim is to show the instructor that you understand the answer to the question. For ease of grading, instructors appreciate clear, legible answers.

Long Essay Questions

Read the Questions Carefully

Long-answer essay questions usually want you to write at length about several subjects. Read the question carefully to make certain you understand exactly what the instructor wants you to include in your answer. Some students misunderstand the main purpose of a question and meander off into other areas. The reasons Napoleon lost the battle at Waterloo are primarily military. An analysis of his personality wastes time and earns no points.

Outline Answers

Outline your answer to a long-answer essay question before writing it. In this way you will ensure that you include key ideas for which you will earn points from the grader. The procedure saves time in the long run. You can organize your answer and can be sure to include everything that is important. You will feel more organized when you begin to write and will have few uncertainties about whether you have included everything you should.

Use an Introduction

Begin by describing the most important questions you intend to answer or the main ideas you intend to discuss in your essay. It can help to pretend that you are writing a short article and need an interesting opening.

Define Terms

Define the terms that you use in your answer. Be sure to call attention to conflicting viewpoints or any uncertainties in your mind about the questions asked. This approach often clarifies for the instructor why you have answered the question in a particular manner.

Use Subheadings

As you write, be sure to use subheadings for longer answers. Subheadings show you and the reader the organization in your answer. Notice how this section, Long-Answer Essay Questions, uses many subheadings. Imagine how difficult this page would be to read without them!

Use Examples and Facts

It is crucial to use examples to support your main points. You demonstrate that you really know what you are talking about if you can present examples to substantiate your position. Include facts, numbers, and details. Be specific. Instead of writing, "Every student needs friends," write, "According to

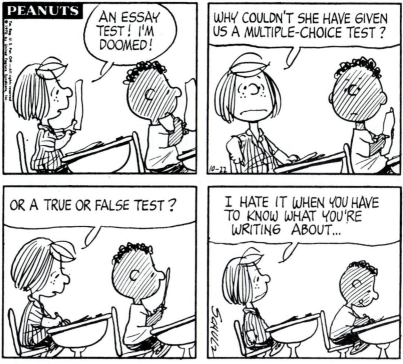

Reprinted by permission of UFS, Inc.

Maslow, it is easier for a student who feels accepted by others to engage in personal growth and self-development than for a student who doesn't feel well accepted."

Draw Conclusions

Summarize and draw conclusions. Be definite and positive. But note, do not include any new data, points, or examples in the conclusion. Add new questions, perhaps, but no new information.

Edit Answers

Above all, write legibly! After you have finished writing, pretend that you are the grader. Ask yourself, "Have I misread or misinterpreted the questions? What did I leave out? Have I made any careless mistakes?" Allot time at the end to edit your answers for clarity, add necessary points, and deal with more difficult questions that you skipped over.

Questions You Didn't Think You Could Answer

What can you do when you come to a question that baffles you? Try to remember that in your reading you're likely to have picked up some information that is relevant. Write down anything that is a possibility. You may earn a few points. A few points is more than you'll earn if you leave the answer blank.

A Sample Test About Tests

Here is a short quiz that illustrates the kinds of tests we've just described.

1. This kind of test item is a
   a. test of recall.
   b. true-false item.
   c. multiple choice item.
   d. all of the above.

2. Multiple-choice tests
   a   have you choose the correct answer from different possibilities.
   b. are more common than true-false tests.
   c. are tests of recognition.
   d. all of the above.

3. T   F   This is a true-false test item.

4. T   F   True-false items are a test of recall.

5. Match the items in the first list with items in the second list:

   __a. True-false   1. Most common recognition test

   __b. Short answer essay   2. 50 percent chance of guessing right

   __c. Multiple choice   3. Test of recall

6. A test that requires you to fill in a missing word or phrase is a test of your ability to _____ a correct answer.

7. Name and give examples of two different types of tests given to college students

ANSWERS: 1. c; 2. d; 3. T; 4. F; 5. a-2, b-3, c-1; 6. recall; 7. Recognition tests: multiple choice, true-false, matching. Recall tests: short written answers, long essays, fill-in.

While taking the exam, you're likely to pick up some information related to the answer you need. If you can't figure out the exact answer, you can probably figure out an approximation. In math, for example, you may work out problems and come up with incorrect answers. You may not receive complete credit, but partial credit is surely better than a zero. Instructors often review the process you used to solve a problem and award points for what you did correctly.

Using your imagination takes practice and even a little confidence. It is not the most important study skill that we can recommend, but using it can be valuable at times.

Strategies to Try that You May Have Never Thought About

Write Comments About the Test

If, in spite of all your excellent preparation, you are still a bit nervous about the test, try imagining that written across the top is the statement, "Feel free to write comments about the test items."

Wilbert J. McKeachie, a psychologist well known for his research on ways to improve teaching, discovered that when this statement was printed at the top of tests, many students did better. The students who were helped most were those who had stronger than average fears of failing. An interesting result was that it didn't matter whether students actually wrote anything about the test! Just the presence of the statement was enough to improve the scores of students who had strong fears of failing.

So, when you are taking a test, remember that you should *feel free to write comments about the test items.* If you believe that a question is poorly worded, say so. But also go on to explain why and perhaps suggest a better wording. The whole purpose of the examination is to show that you know something about the subject. Note: If you have doubts about being allowed comments on the questions, ask!

Ask Questions During the Exam

Instructors know that their questions are not always clear. Sometimes the wording isn't as accurate as it should be. That's why most instructors will answer questions about test questions during exams.

Take advantage of this willingness. If there are one or two questions that just don't make sense, go ask the instructor such questions as, "I am a little confused by this question. Could you give me some assistance?" "The way this item is worded, couldn't there be several possible answers, this one and this one?" "I saw all the films but don't remember the one that this was covered in. Can you give me any clues?"

If you are drawing a blank anyway, you have nothing to lose by seeing whether or not the instructor will give you some hints. He or she will not give you the answer, but a comment like "That item is from the chart at the end of Chapter 6" may give you the clue you need. Try it. Asking the instructor for clues can be worth several extra points on every exam.

The Advantages of These Test-Taking Strategies

When you use the strategies described in this chapter you become more confident about taking tests and you achieve more points on any given test. When taking tests, you will find that you don't make those unfortunate mistakes that make you want to kick yourself and ask, "Why didn't I use my brain?"

You will read the questions carefully, plan your time well, determine the value of specific questions, and answer questions in ways likely to earn the maximum number of points. You will use test-taking strategies we most often observe in students who comprehend their course material and do well on exams. In essence, you will be a more successful student and will still have time for friends.

Experience proves that students who use these techniques seldom:

1. misread the test questions and answer questions incorrectly

2. waste time on questions that stump them

3. waste time answering questions with information they know is irrelevant

4. run out of time and fail to complete the test

5. lose points as a result of changing their answers at the last minute

6. have difficulty answering questions that they didn't think they could answer

7. develop exam panic when a test appears more difficult than they had predicted

8. fail tests (they usually receive B or better).

Students who use these techniques report that they:

1. get better grades on tests

2. receive more points for answers than they would have predicted

3. feel more relaxed and confident while taking tests

4. know they haven't wasted their time while answering complex as well as simple questions

5. feel better organized while taking tests

6. seldom leave out important information from answers

7. are able to complete exams in the allotted time

8. Get higher grades in their courses.

NOTE: It is not necessary to play the "suffering student" game. Learning can be pleasant. Studying for exams can be efficient if you use the strategies we've discussed. If you prepare well for exams, the night before each exam you can relax and do one more very helpful thing: *Get a good night's sleep!*

❏ **ACTION REVIEW: Checklist for Success in Preparing For and Taking Tests**

___ Do I practice quizzing myself on possible test questions?

___ Do I make up and take practice tests?

___ Do I exchange practice tests with other students in the class?

___ Do I practice taking tests under conditions as similar as possible to those under which I will be tested?

___ When I take tests, do I use the techniques suggested in this chapter?

___ Have I made an effort to learn from successful students how they study and take tests?

❏ **ACTION GUIDELINES: Review an "A" Essay Exam**

One of the best ways to learn how to succeed is to look at the products of people you want to emulate. One of the strategies we have found most useful to help students learn test-taking skills is to review and evaluate essay tests by other students who have received high marks.

We first recommend that you borrow several copies of "A" essay exams from friends, classmates, or instructors. Then use the following checklist to evaluate the test.

___ Does the introduction include the key ideas that will be covered in the answer? Is it clear which questions will be answered in the essay?

___ Are the terms and concepts clearly defined? Does it appear that the student got extra points for highlighting all the important terms and concepts?

___ Does each paragraph have a central idea? Is the central idea supported and illustrated with examples to prove the point being made in the paragraph?

___ Does the conclusion successfully summarize the main points made in the essay?

SUCCESS GROUP ACTIVITY: Interview Several Students Who Get "A" Grades on Examinations

A productive group activity is to invite several "A" students to meet with you to explain what they know about taking examinations. Ask them to tell you about their strategies for taking each kind of test.

It is important to hear students that you respect put into their own words what they do when they take tests. By comparing and contrasting their strategies, you will gain valuable insights into strategies for taking all kinds of tests.

9

Writing "A" Papers: How to Use the Library Well

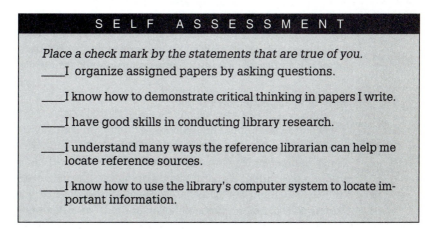

S E L F   A S S E S S M E N T

Place a check mark by the statements that are true of you.

____I organize assigned papers by asking questions.

____I know how to demonstrate critical thinking in papers I write.

____I have good skills in conducting library research.

____I understand many ways the reference librarian can help me locate reference sources.

____I know how to use the library's computer system to locate important information.

How to Write "A" Papers Easily

The successful way to write papers closely parallels the steps you take in preparing for and taking tests. Begin by asking the following questions when writing a paper for an instructor: "What important questions should I answer in this paper? What are important issues I need to cover in order to demonstrate critical thinking skills?"

Students willing to approach writing from this perspective have found the process to be less difficult and less time consuming. More important, their papers are precise, accurate, and well received by instructors.

Here are the steps to follow for planning and preparing your papers.

Pick Your Topic

Pick a topic you find interesting and that your instructor believes is important. By listening closely in class, you will often detect certain areas that are the instructor's favorites. Our students have found it best to choose topics that they and their instructors have enjoyed researching and reading about.

Instructors can supply bibliographies and other information about their favorite subjects. It may be helpful to talk with them after class or make appointments to discuss your planned paper. Talking with the instructor will give you added insights on the advisability of writing in specific areas. It is also a good way to get to know your instructor.

When you have an assigned paper to write, our suggestion is that you prepare by selecting at least three possible topics. Have a preferred topic, of course, but have several alternative topics that you would find interesting in case the first one proves to be unworkable. Make an appointment to talk with your instructor about your proposed topics. If you ask good questions during your discussion, it is amazing how often the instructor will suggest many approaches, useful ideas, critical issues, and key concepts to include. A good discussion can almost outline how your paper should be written. During this discussion, your instructor can also warn you about certain problems to avoid and which issues are either too simple or too complicated to attempt.

Remember Your Audience

Always keep in mind that you are writing to an audience of one person, your instructor. You are not writing an article for the Saturday Review or for your school paper. You are not writing a paper which will be published in a professional journal. Because your instructor is the person you are writing for, it is very important to take extra time to find out exactly what you need to do in your paper to get a good evaluation. If your instructor is vague or unwilling to talk with you about what you plan for your paper, talk to students who have taken the course in the past. Try to read papers that other students have written for this instructor to gain an idea about what was liked and disliked.

List Important Questions, Cover Different Perspectives

Brainstorm a list of important questions you should answer in the paper. To demonstrate critical thinking, come up with questions that examine the subject from more than one view and cover the pros and cons of each view.

Your list will help you determine whether your topic is too broad or too narrow. Too often students find that they would have to produce encyclopedias to cover all relevant questions adequately. If you limit yourself to a few important questions, you will be in a better position to relax as you do the research and writing.

Begin your paper by indicating that you intend to deal only with specific questions and critical issues. Be humble and indicate that you recognize that there may be other significant questions, but that you have chosen to limit yourself to several high-priority questions.

What if my instructor says I have missed an important issue? What do I do then?

We stress talking with your instructor to determine whether or not the questions and critical issues that you think are important are the ones the instructor would like answered.

What if I'm in a class of 200 and don't have access to the instructor or teaching assistant?

You have several alternatives. Many schools provide students with a writing skills center. If you put into practice the recommendation in Chapter 2 about acquainting yourself with your campus, you should know where writing help is available. Take advantage of this useful *free* service! It is there for all writers, no matter their skill level.

Go to the library. Find a *reference librarian*. Reference librarians are wonderful people to know. They can help you find sources of information you probably wouldn't think of. They know the library thoroughly and can be extremely helpful.

Skim through the most recent books and journals that deal with your topic. Even new books can be several years behind the times, so it is wise to go to journals that are more up to date. By looking at what the experts are doing, you are likely to get a better idea of the important questions currently being investigated.

Discuss your topic with students majoring in the subject. They may be aware of important questions that you have overlooked. Once you have a list of good questions, the next step is to develop an outline of your paper.

Develop an Outline

Now that you have a list of questions, take a minute to develop an overall picture of your paper. Try outlining the paper. First will be your introduction. Sketch out one. An introduction is usually one or two paragraphs. It tells your instructor which important questions you intend to answer. By stating the main points you'll be making, you will focus the reader's attention. He or she will know what to look for. Don't worry about your introduction being perfect. It may change dramatically after you have answered your questions. Just sketch an introduction that will lead you in the right direction.

Next, list in order the questions you will be answering. Make sure your questions are listed in a logical sequence. The last part of your outline will be the conclusion. At this point, you haven't answered your questions, so you won't be in a position to draw any conclusions. Your outline will include:

a rough draft of your introduction

the body of your paper—the questions you intend to answer, the critical issues you intend to cover

a statement about writing a conclusion after you have researched your questions.

Talk to Your Instructor

After you have developed an outline, you need to ensure that you are going in the right direction. Make an appointment with your instructor. It will take the instructor only a few seconds to scan your outline to see if you are focusing on the important questions and issues. He or she may give you a few hints about other questions you may wish to answer. Now, off to the library to find answers.

How to Use Your Library Well

Libraries are wonderful places. In libraries you can discover extraordinary ideas, amazing information, and new worlds. You can find facts to support impressions you have, or data that disprove opinions you don't like. To have these experiences, it is important to know how to use a library.

To use your library well, as we've said before, feel free to ask the librarians for assistance. Think of the librarians as resources. They are paid to help students. More important, librarians want to be sure that every student gets the most possible from the library facilities. Whenever you have a question about using the library, don't be hesitant. Any question you have is a good one. The only poor question is the one you fail to ask.

At some colleges the library offers a credit course on how to use the library. If such a course is available, it would be extremely valuable to take it.

Locating Books

The books housed in the library will be listed in the card catalog, the microfiche system, or the on-line catalog in the library computer system. The card catalog, of course, is the old system used by libraries for many decades. Information about each book is typed onto a 3 by 5-inch card and filed in drawers.

Microfiche is a piece of photographic film usually 4 by 6 inches. It contains information greatly reduced in size, so it has to be magnified for reading. One microfiche sheet replaces dozens of catalog cards. It saves space, is cheaper to produce, and can be updated quickly. To use the microfiche, you sit down at a magnifier, insert the card, and find the items you are looking for.

The on-line computer catalog is in the library's computer system. It is updated almost daily and may even show if a book has been placed on reserve or has been checked out. Through the computer system your library will be linked to a computer network to regional and national libraries. Once in a while you may have to request that a book be sent to you through interlibrary loan.

Let's say your paper is going to be about nutrition and athletic performance. You've heard about high-protein diets and carbohydrate loading and seen ads for Gatorade. You've heard about professional athletes on vegetarian diets. How do you find the facts?

With your questions in mind, you'll probably want to start with the subject index. Libraries index their books in three ways: by *author, subject,* and *title.*

Use your imagination when looking through the subject index. Look under every topic you can think of—nutrition, dieting, physical education, health science, and so on. Make notes of book titles and authors and always write down the complete call number of the book. The call number is the library's code number which tells you exactly where the book is shelved.

If a book has the statement "reference" or "reference desk," you will not find the book in the open shelves. An instructor has probably placed the book on reserve so that no one can check it out of the library. If you go to the reference desk, they will probably let you have the book for several hours and, in some cases, for several days. At some libraries you can check out a reference book at closing time if you return it promptly first thing in the morning.

Finding Periodicals and Journals

After identifying books related to your subject, look at the library's list of periodicals. As with books, there may be a card index, a microfiche index, or a computer index. Most up-to-date information, especially scientific reports on research, appears in professional journals long before it is reported in books. Flip through the lists, looking for titles of journals that could contain articles related to your topic. For your paper you'd cover all the nutrition and physical education journals.

The journals of national professional groups are often titled *The American...* or *National Society of...* or *The Journal of the American...* So be sure to look under "American," "National," and "Journal" in the alphabetical listings.

As you record call numbers for books and the journals, you will begin to see a pattern. The books and journals with relevant information are clustered in two or three places in the library. By going to these sections, you will discover other books and journals that you didn't see in the catalog indexes.

Read first to get a general orientation. When you find useful data or passages you may want to quote in your paper, be very accurate in your recording. It can be very frustrating later, back at your typewriter, not to remember which author you quoted or if the statement in your notes is one of your own obser-vations rather than a quote. Most libraries have coin-operated photocopying equipment available. Save time by using it.

From the journal articles you will learn which authors are most highly re-garded and most frequently cited as experts, and you will get clues about books to look for. Some professional journals publish book reviews of the latest books. You may learn about a book before the library purchases it. In such cases you may have to go to instructors in that area to see if one of them has purchased the book and will allow you to borrow it.

From the books you will learn about which journals focus on your topic most frequently. You may learn about an older journal article that is exactly what you are after. You may discover, for example, that several articles on blood sugar and endurance have been published in medical journals. Thus, an-other area of information opens up to you.

Finding Reference Materials

You still haven't used your library well, however, if you ignore another source of useful information: the reference section. In the reference section you will find many resources, such as encyclopedias. Of most interest right now, however, is the *Reader's Guide to Periodical Literature.*

This index lists in alphabetical order the titles of articles published in the major popular magazines. If an article on nutrition and athletic performance has appeared in *Time*, *Saturday Review*, *Psychology Today*, *Sports Illustrated*, or *Runner's World*, the *Reader's Guide* will list it. Some physicians and sci-entific researchers publish directly in popular publications, so don't discount magazines as a source of information. Besides, the information is usually eas-ier to understand than it is in professional journals and books.

Use almanacs as well. Almanacs can sometimes provide historical facts, statistics, names, and dates not available in encyclopedias or other sources.

Don't overlook the electronic technology, however. Your library may sub-scribe to the *Magazine Index*, available in microfilm, or *Newsbank*, on micro-fiche. In addition, it may subscribe to such computer information networks as *Dialog* or *Datatimes*. Some reference information is now available on com-pact disc and video disc. The modern college library has a wealth of informa-tion available if you learn how to gain access to it!

Using Other Libraries

Explore other libraries in your area. Sometimes city or county libraries have books which the college libraries do not have. Other colleges in your area may have references which you cannot find in your own library on campus. You can use any library nearby, even the medical school library if there happens to be one in your vicinity. These other libraries may not allow you to check books out, but there is no problem in walking in and using any materials they have.

You'll soon discover that by knowing the questions you want to answer, you can quickly cut through the massive amount of material that could otherwise distract you. By reading to answer your questions, you save precious hours that might otherwise be lost in meandering around, wondering how much you should include in your paper.

Writing Your Paper

Write Your Answers

Gathering your information is likely to be the most time-consuming part of writing the paper. Once you have the necessary information, it is time to write the answers to your questions.

Write the answers to your questions as precisely as possible. Be brief. Don't include irrelevant information that clouds the issue. Make your point, back it with sufficient examples and data, and leave it at that.

Give precise references to your information sources in footnotes and in your bibliography. Provide all the information a reader needs to go to the specific publication and find the exact pages referenced.

Answers to questions are more believable when they are precise and well documented. Let your reader know that you've done research on the answers. Quote experts in the field. The more authoritative your examples, the better you will be able to convince your reader. But don't overdo it. Several good examples are all that you need to prove your point.

Brief, accurate quotations are more effective in supporting your points than lengthy quotations or your statements about what other people have said. Brief quotations, figures, and specific facts are more persuasive than vague generalizations.

Arrange Your Answers

Once you have written your answers, arrange them in order so that they build upon one another. Your next task is to connect them by writing the minimum amount of material between each answer. These transitions from answer to answer should be brief.

Rewrite Your Introduction

Now that you have answered your questions and built the body of your paper, you are ready to rewrite your introduction. Many students try to start writing their paper by producing a perfect introduction for their outline. This is a mistake.

Once you have answered your questions, you'll be much better prepared to state exactly what your paper does and does not do. You may have found that several of the questions you originally thought you would answer were less important than other questions you discovered while researching your paper.

Write Your Conclusion

Your conclusion summarizes the major points you have addressed in your paper. You shouldn't include any new data, examples, or information. You may wish to point out that your paper raises further questions that need to be answered at a later date. Essentially, your summary shows how all the pieces fit together to prove a particular point. If the answers to your questions lead to a logical conclusion, you should draw that conclusion and leave it at that.

The Steps So Far

1. Determine which questions you will answer in your paper.
2. Develop an outline for your paper. Write an introduction describing the intent of your paper and the questions you will answer.
3. Ask your instructor to scan your outline.
4. Answer each question as precisely and authoritatively as possible. Provide examples to support your position.
5. Document your sources in footnotes and a bibliography.
6. Put your answers in sequence so that they build upon one another.
7. Provide transitions from answer to answer.
8. Rewrite your introduction.
9. Write your conclusion.

Rewrite Your Paper

After you write your first draft, make an appointment to go over it with your instructor. Most instructors are willing to help you and will give you good feedback about whether you are ready for the typewriter or need to do more research.

Revising is where the real writing of any paper takes place. Most writers produce several rough drafts before attempting their final version. Plan from the beginning to produce a rough draft that you will then revise into your final copy. This way you can produce your first rough draft much more quickly and won't be wasting time by trying to edit, correct typing mistakes, and so on.

When you are in a position to rewrite your paper, you should

1. Have your instructor look over your rough draft.
2. Make sure you have clearly indicated which questions you will answer and critical issues you will discuss.

3. Check to see that your transitions flow smoothly from answer to answer.

4. Vary the length of your sentences. Most of the writing in journals and research books is composed of long, involved, complicated sentences. Such sentences are typical of the way that academics think and talk. Long sentences do not make interesting reading, however. On the other hand, you don't want to make your writing style too simple. The best approach is to mix both long and short sentences.

5. Correct any grammatical, punctuation, or spelling errors.

6. Rewrite or refine any answers.

7. Finish the paper with concluding comments and remarks. Include in this section statements about what you learned in the process of writing the paper. State why writing the paper was a valuable experience for you. Also include questions, if any, that writing this paper has raised in your mind.

Good Effort and Learning

The grade given for a paper is influenced by four questions in the back of the instructor's mind:

1. Did the student put effort into this paper or was it written with the minimum possible effort?

2. Did the student learn anything or is this paper just a collection of words?

3. Is the paper original or has it been plagiarized?

4. Was this paper purchased from a paper writing service?

If you can arrange to do so, glance through a number of term papers. Certain quick impressions will begin to emerge. Some students turn in papers that show very little effort. You don't have to be an instructor to see that such students are trying to get away with the absolute minimum commitment of time, effort, and involvement.

Some students do more work, but they lack involvement with the topic. Their approach is to check out all the books they can on the subject, sit down the night before the paper is due, and put together lists of quotations: "In 1937, C.S. Johnson said.... His view was criticized by Smith, who said..., by Brown who said..., by Jones who said.... But then in Eggland's 1949 book...." Such a paper shows no learning.

Once in a while, a student will copy long passages from a book or article and will turn in the paper without mentioning the author's name or the source of the quotation. Does this approach succeed? Rarely. An article written by an expert on a subject is not like a paper written by a student attempting to learn a subject. And frankly, most instructors can spot the style and point of view in the paper as having come from a certain author.

It's human nature to consider taking shortcuts, but some efforts to save time involve high risks. The probability is high that the payoff will be the opposite of what is desired. That's why asking and answering questions works so well. An instructor reading your paper can see that your work is *original*, that you put *good effort* into it, and that you have *learned* something. Remember, an experienced instructor will usually be able to recognize exactly what you do or don't do in preparing your paper.

Some students resort to purchasing a paper written by someone else. Don't do this. One of the main benefits from going to college is the maturity and self-confidence you gain from handling tough challenges. Besides, instructors are becoming more experienced at spotting papers not written by their students. If you get caught you will be in serious trouble.

Demonstrate Critical Thinking

What does critical thinking mean to you? Does it mean to be highly critical of what someone has said or written? Not to college instructors.

One of the best ways to understand critical thinking is to ask "What is the opposite of critical thinking?" When students describe uncritical thinking they say that it means to:

"Accept without reservation what someone is saying."

"Believe whatever is told to you is the truth."

"Not want to listen to another explanation or perspective."

"Believe that the thinking of one person or group is entirely right and good while the thinking of opposing persons or groups is bad and wrong."

To demonstrate critical thinking in a paper means to ask and answer questions that provide more than one perspective, viewpoint, or explanation *and* to discuss the strong points and weak points of each perspective. Your aim is to demonstrate that you can think in critical ways even about a theory, method, philosophy, or school of thinking that you like.

Grammar, Spelling, and Neatness

One final set of suggestions is important. Determine whether your instructor requires that you keyboard your papers. You can safely assume that the instructor prefers it, for most instructors do. Handwritten papers are difficult to read. They slow down the instructor and cause eye strain. Your instructor reads hundreds of articles, books, and papers every year. It is a sign of consideration to present your writing in the most readable form. Make your printed copy as professional as possible. Use clean white paper, double-space the lines, and make a minimum number of corrections on the printed copy.

Always be careful to follow any directions your instructor gives for footnotes, bibliographies, references, or other requirements. There is nothing worse than devoting hours to a paper only to have it returned as incomplete. The consequences of failing to follow directions can be costly.

It can be a challenge to follow the requirements assigned by your instructors. It may be one of the small sacrifices you have to make as a student. You may be dismayed to find that what your instructor wants for the form of a paper contradicts what your English instructor taught you to do. In the end, however, you'll probably find out that there's a good reason for your instructor's request. Go along with the suggestions and you will usually be better off, both in the grade you receive and the level of your blood pressure after completing the paper.

Above all, make sure that your spelling is accurate. Use a dictionary whenever you are in doubt. If you have problems in this area and are using a computer, be sure to remind yourself to run the spellchecker. It would also be wise to have someone check your paper for grammatical mistakes. Regardless of the quality of your ideas, there are few things that bother instructors more than poor spelling and bad grammar.

It has been shown in several studies that instructors usually grade papers higher when the papers are neat and clean and when they include good spelling and good grammar.

NOTE: Always keep a copy of your paper. The original could get damaged or lost. Some instructors keep papers. Play it safe. Keep a copy on disk and a hard copy for yourself before turning in the original.

Some Important Tip s

In working with college students, there are some things we have observed that will help you. *First*, after you have written a rough draft, read aloud what you have written. Students often fail to pick up obvious mistakes because through silent reading they miss things that would be obvious if they were to read their papers aloud.

Second, get someone else to read the paper to see if it makes sense. Listening to feedback from another person about your writing is often painful. But it is more painful to hear those same remarks from your instructor. Do the same for your friends. Read their papers. Learn to be a better writer from analyzing the mistakes of others. As you exchange information about one another's writing, be pleasant and give constructive help. Try to encourage one another.

Third, if you have difficulties, go to the writing lab. Get some tutoring. The English department has many helpful graduate students available to show you how to write good papers.

Fourth, the key to the whole thing is to decide that you *want* to develop writing competence. Have you made that decision? Do you want to write well?

Writing skills will help you throughout your entire life, no matter what field you enter. Writing skills can even help you communicate effectively in your personal letters. Take advantage of this opportunity. Aim to become a competent writer and practice whenever you can. You'll never regret it.

Always Do Your Own Work

Many students unintentionally find themselves in a tremendous bind as a result of not knowing exactly what plagiarism is and is not. Plagiarism is a form of stealing. The act of plagiarism occurs when a student copies statements from some source and presents the material to the instructor as being his or her original work. No credit is given to the real author and no quotation marks are used.

Direct plagiarism occurs when a passage is quoted verbatim (word for word). Indirect plagiarism occurs when the student paraphrases the original work without giving credit to the original author. Paraphrasing means to substitute certain words and alter some sentences while repeating all the main ideas. Even though the original work was not copied verbatim, the ideas and substance have been copied.

Another version of plagiarism is to purchase a term paper or report written by someone else. This is a high-risk way of trying to get a passing grade. If the instructor spots the work as not yours, you are in big trouble.

It is also unacceptable to have another student rewrite your papers. Don't do it. Supportive, constructive feedback and fresh thinking on the subject is all right, but don't ask someone to take over and do the work and don't do theirs if they ask.

Plagiarism can cause you serious problems in the academic world. It is grounds for being flunked in a course, referred for counseling, placed on disciplinary probation, or even expelled from the college.

REMEMBER: If you are in doubt about whether you are plagiarizing:
1. See your instructor for guidance.
2. Use quotation marks and footnotes.
3. Make the effort to write what you've read in your own words.

❏ ACTION REVIEW: Checklist for Success in Writing Papers and Using Your Library

	Yes	No	
1.	___	___	Do I write papers using the question and answer format?
2.	___	___	Have I asked the reference librarian for suggestions about where to look for information?
3.	___	___	Do I use the card catalog and microfiche to track down good reference sources?

4. ___ ___ Do I get up-to-date information from professional journals?

5. ___ ___ Do I use the *Reader's Guide* to learn about useful magazine articles?

6. ___ ___ Do I use other libraries in the vicinity?

7. ___ ___ Are my quotes and references accurate?

8. ___ ___ When the rough draft is completed, do I ask the instructor to look it over and give me suggestions for improvement?

9. ___ ___ Do I check to insure that my grammar and spelling are correct?

10. ___ ___ Is my written work clean and readable?

11. ___ ___ After my paper has been graded and returned to me, do I look for ways to improve next time?

❏ ACTION GUIDELINES: Researching Research

1. Go to the library.
2. Locate *The World Book Encyclopedia.*
3. Read the chapter on "How to Do Research" in Volume 22.

SUCCESS GROUP ACTIVITIES

1. Arrange to have one of the librarians show your group how to find the many resources available in the library. By now you have a general understanding, but what more is there to know about the library? Prepare for your special session by listing questions you would like to have answered. Include such questions as, "What don't most students understand about the library's resources?" or "What do you wish students understood better about the library's services?" Find out about learning labs or computer rooms that may be available to you.

2. Read each other's papers. Trying to critique your own papers is one of the most difficult tasks you will face in college. You can read your own paper over and over, not being sure of what you have overlooked or how well you have done. Another person reading it for the first time will spot things you've overlooked.

After you have developed rough drafts of your term papers, talk with each other about the questions that provide the structure for your paper. Give and get positive suggestions from each other about the following: Have you met the goal of the assignment? Are your grammar, spelling, and punctuation acceptable? What would you add or delete to improve the paper? How could the paper be improved without a total rewrite?

NOTE: It can be helpful to summarize your paper to a friend. In giving a summary you will often come up with a better organization than you had for the paper. The summary is usually stronger than the paper itself. By summarizing what you've written, you gain a better idea of the topic and a better flow.

part four

Instructors, Friends, and Family

- ❏   *Myths About Instructors*

- ❏   *How to Improve the Instruction You Receive*

- ❏   *How to Develop Friendships and Gain Support from Your Family*

10

Myths About Instructors

SELF ASSESSMENT

Place a check mark by the statements that are true of you.

_____It is likely that some of my assumptions about my instructors are inaccurate.

_____It is possible that some of my inaccurate assumptions about my instructors will create problems for me.

_____I know that many students have erroneous beliefs about instructors.

_____I know that unrealistic expectations about my instructors can make me angry and disappointed.

_____I know how to change my unrealistic expectations about instructors.

_____I have noticed that some students act as though they want to give a bad impression to instructors and cause negative reactions.

_____I am aware of biases some instructors have toward students.

_____I am aware how students' positive and negative behavior patterns effect their instructors' teaching performance.

_____I am aware how negative student behavior toward instructors can cause negative reactions and hurt the students.

SOME ERRONEOUS ASSUMPTIONS ABOUT INSTRUCTORS

When you accept complete responsibility for learning from your instructors, you're on the right track. You will get more than your money's worth from school. If, however, you assume that your instructors are responsible for you learning everything you want to know, you may become disappointed with your education.

A candid appraisal of instructors and of your assumptions about them will help you understand why many of your assumptions may be inaccurate. When we teach, we sometimes ask students to list their assumptions and expectations about instructors. Then we compare the assumptions and expectations with reality. In the pages that follow, you will be able to discover which of your assumptions and expectations about instructors are erroneous and which are realistic.

In front of each statement you'll find two spaces. Check off whether or not you believe the statement.

We want you to learn about myths which may be affecting your expectations as to what your instructors should be like. Most important, we want to encourage you to stop letting erroneous assumptions set you up to feel angry, disappointed, and discouraged.

After you have read the myths, we'll move on to talk about predictable conflicts between teaching styles and learning styles, some successful ways to gain as much as possible from a variety of different types of instructors, and how to avoid alienating your instructors.

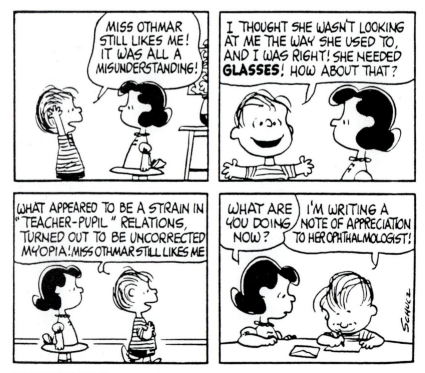

Reprinted by permission of UFS, Inc.

Myths About Instructors

<u>Agree</u> <u>Disagree</u>

_____ _____   **Myth 1**   Most college instructors are trained in how to be effective instructors.

                Reality: Colleges usually assume that a person with a graduate degree in a subject should be able to teach it. Yet, few college instructors have received formal training in how to be effective teachers. New instructors learn how to teach through trial and error during their early years as instructors and assistant professors. Very few instructors receive training for one of their major responsibilities—*teaching!*

_____ _____   **Myth 2**   All of your instructors will be interesting lecturers and devote considerable effort to making the course stimulating and motivating.

                Reality: Most of your college instructors would like to be interesting, stimulating, and motivating lecturers. But, you will find that your instructors vary widely in their ability to maintain your interest. Some of your instructors will be downright boring and uninteresting regardless of how hard they try to maintain your interest. These instructors may still be excellent at presenting the information you want to learn. They are just not entertainers.

_____ _____   **Myth 3**   Your instructors will always be well prepared for each class you attend.

                Reality: Most of your instructors will be well-prepared for each class. Regardless of how well your instructors plan, sometimes a class won't work out as well as they hope. Sometimes instructors' commitments and personal lives get in the way of their planning. They may come to class poorly prepared. Some of your instructors may even get to the point where they feel too confident and do little or no planning.

<u>Agree</u> <u>Disagree</u>

_____ _____   Myth 4   Most instructors will take a personal interest in you.

Reality: Some instructors will want to get to know you as a person and will devote time to you. They will enjoy talking with you after class, around campus, in their offices, and at social or athletic events. Some instructors, however, are so busy that they just don't have much time for students. They are too busy with academic responsibilities, research, writing for publication, teaching classes, and professional activities to have much time for anyone—even their own families. Still others are very private people. They prefer to keep things strictly on a teacher-student basis and do not see that personal interest in students has a place in the classroom.

_____ _____   Myth 5   University and college instructors have little personal interest in students and should not be asked for assistance if a course is too difficult.

Reality: Many students are so awed by an instructor who has been transformed into a prestigious noun, such as "doctor" or "professor," that they assume such an instructor will have little interest or concern for a lowly student. Impressive titles and offices heaped with books and papers do tend to create distance between instructors and students, but most instructors are available and enjoy contact with students sincerely motivated to learn. Unfortunately, many students who could use help in a course do not seek assistance because of erroneous beliefs about instructors' attitudes.

_____ _____   Myth 6   Instructors want most ideas challenged and want students to present their opinions and views during class.

<u>Agree</u> <u>Disagree</u>

Reality: Many instructors will seek as much appropriate and useful student input as possible. A small proportion will have little or no interest in students' opinions and views. Other instructors will feel that they have limited time to present vast amounts of important information. These instructors are often rather dedicated individuals who don't wish to offend students but very often discourage student input so as to maintain their schedules. For such instructors, getting through the course material is more important than letting students express their views.

_____ _____   Myth 7   The instructor's coverage of the course material will be nonjudgmental, unbiased, objective, and comprehensive.

Reality: Many instructors use teaching as a way to advocate and promote their personal perspectives on their subject. They tend to play up why their approaches, conclusions, and methods are correct and the views and teachings of some other people in the field are wrong. A few instructors make it clear in their reactions to questions about opposing views or the works of certain people that such ideas or works are not worthy of attention.

_____ _____   Myth 8   Instructors want you to accept obediently everything they say without reservation and be able to regurgitate accurately on exams the truths they've taught.

Reality: Most instructors have two goals. One is for you to understand the basic facts and concepts in the field or subject being taught. The other is for you to learn to think for yourself. Once you understand these two goals, you can learn the content of the course and at the same time question basic assumptions.

<u>Agree</u> <u>Disagree</u>

_____   _____   Myth 9   Your instructors will be pleasant people.

Reality: Many of your instructors will be people who have entered the teaching profession because they enjoy having a positive effect on other people. These instructors will often be pleasant to be around and have a profound effect on their students. A small proportion of your instructors will be neither pleasant nor unpleasant. These instructors will simply be there to help you learn. A very small proportion of your instructors will be irritable, unpleasant, and bores to be around. If you are asking the question, "Do I like this instructor?" you are asking the wrong question. The right question is, "Does this teacher know the subject well enough to teach me something?"

_____   _____   Myth 10   Your instructors will be able to answer all of your questions about the subject.

Reality: Most instructors see education as an ongoing process for themselves as well as for their students. Being well educated includes learning what you don't know. Being well educated is to discover that some answers are partially true or only correct in certain circumstances.

Would you rather have an instructor who can give you what seems to be a definite, correct answer about everything or one who says, once in a while, "I don't know," and then suggests a way to find the answer?

One of the results when you ask good questions and learn what the answers are is that you eventually run out of people who can answer your questions. Questions which no one can answer well are the forerunners of new knowledge, scientific advances, and exciting career directions.

Agree Disagree

_____ _____   Myth 11   Your instructors will know more than you.

        Reality: If you've had a thirst for knowledge for many years, read a lot, and learned from life's experiences, you may find that you know more about some things than the instructor does. As disappointing as this may be to you, the fact is that you may be too advanced for the class. If so, is that a legitimate excuse for being angry at the instructor or the school?

        One of the signs of having an educated heart as well as an educated mind is that you can handle those times when you discover that someone with an advanced degree knows less about a topic than you. And if you think you understand the topic so well, how about taking your turn as a teacher? Are you ready for that?

_____ _____   Myth 12   Your instructor must have firsthand experience to be able to teach a subject well.

        Reality: In trade schools, experience is essential. There are many courses, however, where the sniping comments, such as "How can he know, he's never been there," only serve to rationalize not listening. An instructor in management can teach many practical ideas without ever having owned or run a business. A person can teach child development well without having had children. A psychologist can teach about mental disturbances without having been a mental patient. History teachers can teach well without having "been there."

        Firsthand experience is very useful, but not essential. In fact, many people with experience don't know how to teach what they do. Have you ever tried to learn from Granny exactly how she makes that special dessert the family loves? Asking "has the instructor had firsthand experience" is asking the wrong question. Asking, "Can this instructor teach well?" is a better question.

DEVELOPING REALISTIC ATTITUDES

Being angry or disappointed because of your inaccurate predictions about the behavior of your instructors can only hinder your success in college. By dispelling myths about your instructors, learning to predict accurately their behavior, and accepting instructional behavior you had not predicted, you'll avoid setting yourself up to feel victimized.

Developing realistic attitudes and strategies for coping with instructors' behavior may be an important step in increasing your happiness and success in college. The action projects at the end of this chapter will provide you with guidelines for dispelling myths and developing realistic attitudes about your instructors. You will see how changing your actions toward your instructors may enhance your success in the classroom and general happiness in college.

YOUR EMOTIONAL HABITS AFFECT YOUR SUCCESS IN SCHOOL

When we talk to students about the myths versus the realities of college instructors, we hear disgusted, angry, impassioned, and sometimes humorous stories of students' feelings for and against instructors. There is no question that your instructors' personalities and teaching behaviors will have a profound impact on your attitude toward learning and your performance in college.

What does all this mean for you? The reality of going to college is that you'll attend courses taught by instructors with just about every personality characteristic imaginable. You'll attend courses taught by highly competent instructors and less competent instructors. That is simply the way things work. Any student can learn something in a class taught by an excellent instructor. It takes an excellent student to learn well in a class taught by a less competent instructor or one not tuned into your style of learning.

Remember, you are responsible for your learning. How well you do is up to you. *Learning is the game, not teaching.*

As you will see in more detail in Chapter 14, you can make your attitudes work for you or against you. You can attempt to get the most possible out of every course, regardless of your instructors' personalities or levels of competency. Or you can complain and moan about your instructors and blame them for why you are not learning anything. It is all up to you!

❏ **ACTION GUIDELINES: Dispelling a Myth**

The way you react when an instructor doesn't live up to your expectations determines how good an education you will get. When you are disappointed, do you get mad at the instructor and the school, or do you find a way to make the course work for you?

1.   Look at the list of myths. Select one that you agreed with, and challenge yourself to dispel that myth. Focus your attention on the reality of your instructors by answering these questions:

> Are my thoughts and beliefs about each instructor based on actual experience, or do they come from past experiences with other teachers and statements made by other students?

> Why is it reasonable and legitimate for instructors to be as they are even though I may be disappointed or upset?

> Can I learn something from an instructor who is less than ideal—who has weaknesses, flaws, and limitations?

2.   How could you go about changing the habits and attitudes that are based on your assumptions? What would be the benefit to you?

3.   Set a goal to dispel a myth in which you believe. Describe what you would do on a daily basis for the next month to demonstrate to yourself how erroneous your assumptions have been.

4.   A month from now, come back to this space and write in exactly what you did over the past month to change your habits and attitudes. How did you dispel the myth?

SUCCESS GROUP ACTIVITIES

1.   Discuss erroneous beliefs you have had about your instructors and how certain myths may be having a negative effect on your adjustment to college. What expectations did you have about college that have not been borne out? How have your false expectations created a problem for you? How can you work around it?

2.   Do you have negative expectations about college that have not been borne out to date? If at some later point your negative expectation begins to appear to be true, how can you prevent it from hindering your performance as a student?

3.   Have you noticed how you act when an expectation you have turns out to be untrue? Do you become upset? Angry? Depressed? Why do people become upset when their expectations are unfulfilled? How can you overcome this problem? Spend time discussing these issues. Your friends will often provide insights that are far more astute or beneficial than those of a trained counselor.

4.   Compare your lists of how you could create a negative impression on an instructor if you actively set out to do so. Do the lists increase your self-awareness? Can you see how you and other students can sometimes create a negative reaction in instructors without knowing what you are doing?

5.   Talk about what actions you can take to avoid causing negative reactions and to create more positive impressions on instructors.

11

How to Improve the Instruction You Receive

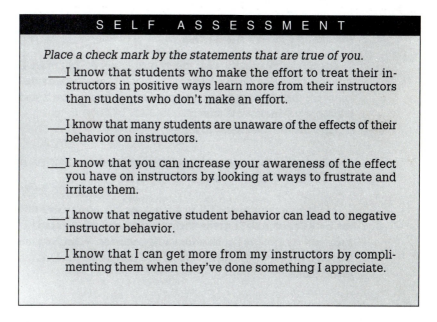

SELF ASSESSMENT

Place a check mark by the statements that are true of you.

___I know that students who make the effort to treat their instructors in positive ways learn more from their instructors than students who don't make an effort.

___I know that many students are unaware of the effects of their behavior on instructors.

___I know that you can increase your awareness of the effect you have on instructors by looking at ways to frustrate and irritate them.

___I know that negative student behavior can lead to negative instructor behavior.

___I know that I can get more from my instructors by complimenting them when they've done something I appreciate.

HELPING YOUR INSTRUCTORS BE BETTER INSTRUCTORS

If you say to yourself, "It's my job to help my instructor do well!" you can have a profound effect on your instructor's performance. There are many things you can do as a student to make the lives of your instructors more pleasant and their performance more useful to you.

Make Sure the Instructor Knows You

No matter how large the class, find some way to introduce yourself and let the instructor know why this course is important to you. Make an effort to have the instructor know you and recognize you. If you have special reasons for taking the course, let the instructor know what they are. Instructors need to know you are interested and motivated to learn from them.

Reward Your Instructors for Good Teaching

When your instructors do something that you consider to be effective teaching, let them know that you appreciate it. Rewards for good teaching are few and far between. After a better-than-average lecture, tell your instructor what you liked about it. Most students are reluctant to compliment their instructors because they don't want to appear to be apple polishers. Your instructors will probably be excellent judges of sincere comments and will appreciate what you have to say. Don't hold back your compliments. Let your instructors know you like their teaching.

Develop a Positive Action Plan

Do you know exactly what things instructors do that make them good instructors? Can you clearly describe the specific, observable behaviors that you know are the basis for good teaching? Do you know what a student can do to reinforce and improve teaching?

Here are the basic steps to follow:

Step 1—Take a few minutes to list all those things that good teachers do. List specifics. List observable behaviors.

In the following space fill in a few specific, observable things that good teachers do, such as "Listens attentively when I ask a question." Saying that a teacher "is nice" is not an observable behavior. When you are through, get together with several other students and compare lists. Discuss the lists and revise them.

1. _____

2. _____

3. _____

4. _____

5. _____

6. _____

7. _____

Compare your list to ours. Do you believe there is a consensus among students as to the basic characteristics of good instruction?

Good instructors

clearly define their objectives for the course and each class session

clearly define course grading and testing procedures

encourage students to ask questions and participate in class discussion

answer students' questions during class

present informative and interesting lectures and class discussions

are organized and well prepared

periodically summarize the major points and issues presented in lectures and discussions

are considerate of students and treat them with respect

are able to admit when they are unsure of an answer

demonstrate a willingness to listen to and assess opinions which conflict with their own

are enthusiastic about teaching

provide students with assistance outside of class.

Our list of good instructional behavior is simply a starting point. We want to encourage you to consistently think about what your instructors are doing well. Equally important, we want to encourage you to reward your instructors for good instructional behavior.

Step 2—Brainstorm a list of all the reinforcing things you could do in response to a desired teaching behavior.

To brainstorm means to write out a list of ideas as fast as you can. The emphasis is on quantity, not quality. Be wild and imaginative. Be outrageous and funny. Do this with three or four other people and see how much fun brainstorming can be.

After about five minutes, stop and go through the list to see what things you could do. NOTE: You will continue to come up with ideas for the list for a few more hours, so wait a day or so before finishing your basic list.

1. _____

2. _____

3. _____

4. _____

5. _____

6. _____

7. _____

8. _____

9. _____

Step 3—Type out a copy of your lists of desired teaching behaviors and teacher reinforcers and place it in your notebook.

Step 4—Now look for the first possible opportunity to observe a good teaching behavior and reward it!

Respond Positively to Good Instructional Behavior

When your instructors are doing things which you consider to be good teaching, be very attentive. Nod, even smile. Instructors' actions are determined to a large extent by the attention they receive from students. When you and the other students indicate your approval of your instructor's good teaching behavior, you'll encourage your instructor to do more of the things you like and less of what you don't like.

If you don't see why your body language is important, imagine standing in front of a group of students who are nodding off to sleep, gazing out windows, carrying on private conversations, and generally acting disinterested. Would you be motivated to be enthusiastic and well prepared to teach this group of students?

If you have any doubt about the effect sincere attention and appreciation have on instructors, think about your own experiences. Think about the motivating effects that sincere attention have had on you.

Provide Your Instructors with Feedback

If your instructors encourage periodic evaluations of their classroom performance, be sure to fill out their evaluations. Let your instructors know what you like! If you want to tell an instructor that something needs to be improved, be sure to give an example of what you don't like and what you would like. As an instructor, there are few things worse than having a student tell you to improve some aspect of your teaching behavior but not give you a clear example of what he or she would like you to do. Be sure you can give an example of what you would like to see more or less of (for example, clearer instructions and fewer personal stories).

Help Your Instructor Be Clear and Precise

Encourage your instructors to clearly define their expectations of students. If your instructor is unclear about an assignment, pleasantly ask him or her to re-state it. Don't hesitate to ask for clarification. If you didn't understand the assignment, more than likely, other more timid students are also saying to themselves, "What is it the instructor wants us to do?" You'll be doing yourself, your fellow students, and your instructor a favor by asking for clarification.

Regardless of how unclear an instructor may be, when you ask your clarifying question, don't make a big deal about how confused you are. Don't make instructors look like idiots. Just ask them to clarify what they want and thank them for their help.

If after asking for clarification regarding an assignment you are still confused, don't badger the instructor. Try not to say things like, "I still don't know what you want!" or "You really haven't been clear about the assignment!" More than likely, you and several other students can figure out what your instructor is assigning. If not, step up after class and pleasantly point out your confusion. When you ask for clarification, ask confidently; try not to act bewildered.

Unclear questions from instructors often turn students' stomachs. You're likely to think to yourself, "What is it she's asking?" Don't let your gut reaction show! Pleasantly ask your instructor to restate the question. If your instructor's second attempt isn't any clearer than the first, pleasantly indicate that you're unsure of the answer. Try to avoid throwing your hands into the air and saying, "I don't know what you're getting at!"

Prepare Good Questions Before Going to Class and Always Try to Answer Your Instructor's Questions

As you read your assignments for class, decide what questions you would like your instructor to answer. In class, listen attentively to see if your instructor answers your questions. If not, don't be reluctant to pose your questions to your instructor.

Most instructors want students to ask good questions. Too often, students sit back timidly, afraid to ask questions. Instructors then worry whether the students have any idea as to what's going on.

Instructors prepare lectures hoping to stimulate students' inquisitiveness. If you sit back and fail to ask questions or turn your face to the floor every time an instructor poses a question, both you and the instructor will be losers. Give your instructors opportunities to demonstrate their intelligence: Ask good questions! Give yourself an opportunity to demonstrate your intelligence: Answer your instructor's questions!

Attend All Classes

Instructors work hard to prepare lectures. When you decide to skip a class, you are saying to your instructors, "I don't believe what you are doing is of any value!" Show your instructors by your attendance that you value what they have to say. If you must miss a class, do not show up at the next session and ask, "Did I miss anything important?" Don't remind the instructor that you were absent. Just return to class and find out from a friend or another student what you missed.

Turn In Your Assignments on Time

Late assignments often suggest to your instructors that you lack enthusiasm for their courses. Some instructors reciprocate with a lack of enthusiasm for your procrastination by deducting points from late papers. Do your best to show you care. Don't say it with flowers; say it with papers!

Develop a Flexible Learning Style

The famous psychologist Abraham Maslow once stated that if you have clear goals you can learn from even bad instructors. Recent research into learning styles shows, however, that the problem may not be that the instructor is bad. It may be that there is a mismatch between the instructor's teaching style and your learning style.

Auditory versus Visual

Some people learn best by listening. Others learn best by seeing. An instructor with an auditory preference will talk a lot and not provide much information in writing. If you learn best from reading you may see this instructor as doing a poor job.

If you learn best from what you hear, you get along great with a talkative instructor but not well with one who relies on handouts, assigned readings, and writing on the blackboard.

Left Brain versus Right Brain

The human brain appears to be divided into two halves. In recent years, psychologists have shown that the two halves are so different in their functions that the cerebral cortex can be considered to be two different brains, the left brain and the right brain.

The left brain makes possible logical, analytical ways of talking and thinking. People who rely strongly on their left brain like facts, lists, charts, and objective, unemotional explanations.

The right brain is non-verbal, metaphoric, visual, sensual, and musical. People who function mostly out of their right brains live by the sights, sounds, and feelings of things. They talk with spontaneous, free associations that have no apparent logical connection.

When there is a mismatch between left brain and right brain styles both students and instructors can be upset with each other.

Friendly versus Distant

Instructors and students vary widely in terms of how friendly they want to be with other people and how much emotional distance they need to maintain. If you feel that the instructor is being too friendly or too impersonal take a look at what this reveals about your preferred style.

External versus Internal

In Chapter 3 you learned about ways that people differ in external and internal motivations. An instructor who uses an autocratic, controlling style will have a negative effect on students who are self-motivated. An instructor who uses a style effective with internally motivated students can cause externally motivated students to flounder.

In summary, the problems you experience with instructors will be typical of problems you will encounter throughout life with people you find it difficult to listen to, take direction from, and work with. Some of the best lessons you learn in college are not in assigned course content!

THE GRAND SCHEME: POSITIVE AND NEGATIVE EFFECTS

Students who get better teaching discover that *positive student behavior leads to positive instructor behavior and negative student behavior leads to negative instructor behavior.*

Students seldom claim that reinforcing good teaching will turn an instructor from a Stephen King terrorizer into a Dale Carnegie graduate. But students who actively work to get better teaching are emphatic about the positive effect they can have on an instructor's performance. These students are equally emphatic about the profound negative effect they believe students can have on an instructor's behavior.

Students are wonderful at describing ways to destroy the best of instructors. Some students gleefully relate how they spearheaded a well-planned attack on a high school teacher whom they loathed. Their sadistic glee is often shared by other class members who remember a teacher from high school who found ill-prepared, unmotivated, and uncaring students impossible to tolerate.

Strangely enough, when college students somewhat shamefully list their adolescent behaviors, they often realize what a damaging effect their behavior may have had on that disliked high school instructor. Some high school teachers literally find the inconsiderate, unmotivated, and lackluster students not worth the effort. These unhappy instructors eventually resign themselves to collecting their paychecks and putting up with the daily task of teaching the "ungrateful."

The lot of the college instructor can sometimes be equally disheartening. College professors are known to complain of unmotivated, uncaring, and ill-prepared students. The cause of the professor's distress is often subtle and, it is hoped, unconscious student behavior. In defense of themselves, college students often point out how unaware they are of the effect of their behavior on professors.

As is often the case, people are unaware of the effects of their behavior on others until it is too late. In your case, there has never been a better time to observe the behavior of college students which creates either dedicated and happy professors or those who become frustrated and often uncaring.

It Is a Two-Way Street

Just as positive and negative student behavior leads to positive and negative instructor behavior, the same is true of instructor behavior. Instructors exert a tremendous influence over how students perform in their courses.

Dr. Drew C. Appleby at Marion College did an intriguing study in which he had students interview faculty. The interviews asked instructors to identify the behaviors of students which irritated them. He then asked his students to identify the behaviors of instructors that irritated the students. Appleby reported:

> The purpose of the study was to identify perceptions that negatively affect the teaching/learning process. Certain students behaviors irritate faculty, and specific faculty behaviors irritate students, even though neither of these groups deliberately attempts to irritate the other. Faculty are probably unaware that some of their behavior irritates students, and students may be equally unaware that many of their behaviors irritate teachers. The quality of the teaching/learning environment might be significantly improved if both groups become aware of the impact of these behaviors and decrease their frequency.

The result of these interviews is truly enlightening and should guide both student and instructor behavior. Appleby found that: "(a) teachers are irritated by students who act bored, (b) students are irritated by teachers who are poor communicators, and (c) both groups are irritated by behaviors that they interpret as rude or disrespectful."

There was a clear consensus among faculty about irritating student behaviors. There was an equally clear consensus among students about irritating instructor behaviors. Appleby's research supports the notion that there is a circular causal relationship between student and instructor behavior. When students act negatively, instructors in turn respond to students negatively, which then leads to more negative student behavior. The cycle may go on and on and...

What this research tells us is that we must learn to be aware as students and instructors of the effects of our behavior on one another. Equally important, we must learn to act appropriately toward one another and sense when our behavior is having both positive and negative consequences.

Notice Negative Effects on Your Instructors

As you read the following list of Behaviors Guaranteed to Frustrate Instructors, ask yourself:

> How often have I behaved this way to an instructor?

> What effect would this behavior have on me if I were the instructor?

> If I were the instructor, how would I respond to students who acted in such ways?

By taking the perspective of your instructor, you may discover why it's academic suicide to get caught up in behaving inconsiderately toward your instructors. You may appreciate how easily professors can become disheartened by well-meaning but unthinking students.

BEHAVIORS GUARANTEED TO FRUSTRATE INSTRUCTORS

Argue Angrily with Instructors, Especially over Exams

Students consistently describe instances in which frustrated classmates verbally attack instructors' statements. You have a right to your opinion. But regardless of how seriously you differ with your instructor, you needn't argue. A huffy, heated attack on your instructor's position will gain neither of you anything but a mutual dislike.

USEFUL ALTERNATIVE: Learn to present your difference of opinion assertively but without anger. Ask questions to find out why the differences exist. Turn the conflict into a learning experience.

Treat Classes as Social Hours or as Unwanted Obligations

For a variety of reasons, students often carry on private conversations, act bored, show up late, sleep, leave early, or simply play the fool in class. You wouldn't be paid for sleeping, playing cards, or socializing with your best friend if you were working. Instructors are justified to feel that you don't belong in their courses if you appear to be uninterested in learning.

Be a Know-It-All Student

We've all experienced the know-it-all students who act as though no one has anything of importance to say but them. Know-it-alls are universally disliked. Our students have heard comments directed at know-it-alls such as "Oh, we don't get to hear from you again, do we?" or "You're so smart! You always have the final word!"

USEFUL ALTERNATIVE: If you treat other students as valuable people from whom you can learn, you'll be ahead of the game. Assume that everyone has something of value to say. Acknowledge other students' contributions. If you always try to prove that your instructors and fellow students know less than you, you are only wasting your time.

Tell Emotional and Personal Stories Leading Nowhere

Students often become so involved with class discussions that they go off into personal stories which are typically of little value to anyone. Instructors are just as guilty of overpersonalizing their courses. There are times when our personal experiences are relevant to the focus of class discussion. We simply urge you to always ask yourself, "Will the personal comment I'm going to make add to the class discussion, or do I just want to tell people about myself?"

Periodically, the focus of a class discussion can lead people to become heated, angry, elated, joyous, or just about any emotional state imaginable. When you become emotional in class, if you're like most people, you may have a tendency to allow your mouth to run off with your emotions. Students often define such emotional behavior as "spilling your guts." We've all spilled our guts at times. We're all human. But learn to ask yourself, "Do I really want to say what I am going to say when I feel like this? Do I want to think about what I am responding to and be sure that what I have to say is of value? If I do say something, need I be emotional?"

USEFUL ALTERNATIVE: Learning to think about what you're going to say and why you're going to say it is a skill everyone needs to practice. In your case, the crucial questions are, "Will what I say be of value?" and "How can I say what I want to ensure it will be most useful to other people?"

Expect Your Instructors to Be Outstanding Every Day

All of us have days when we'd prefer to avoid contact with other people. Professors do not have the luxury of hiding in a closet until a bad mood passes. If they haven't had time to prepare for class, they still have to show up.

USEFUL ALTERNATIVE: Show a little compassion. Don't expect the impossible. No one can be outstanding every day. If your professor appears to be having an off day, do your best to make the class a good one. Be more attentive than ever. Ask good questions. Nod and smile at everything your instructor does well. (A word of caution: Don't overdo it. You needn't look like a smiling Cheshire cat. Just be positive.)

After class, if you liked your instructor's performance, go out of your way to say so. It's doubly important on tough days for instructors to know that they can ride out a storm.

Tell Other Students What You Dislike about the Instructor—Never Go Directly to the Instructor

It is easy for you to complain to other students about a particular instructor. The problem is that your complaints won't help your instructor teach better or your classmates learn more. Your complaints may result in students responding negatively toward your instructor, which will surely hurt his or her performance. So why make things tough for your instructor, your fellow students, and yourself?

USEFUL ALTERNATIVE: Encourage other students to get the most out of your instructors' courses. Never downgrade your instructors to other students. Try to help your instructors, not hurt them! Encourage yourself and other students to look for the good points in your instructors. As we've stated throughout this chapter, try to create a climate in which your instructors can do an even better job.

If you decide that you just don't have the time or interest to help your instructors improve their performance, at least keep your negative comments to yourself. Don't make other students suffer who are willing to try to help your instructors.

Be Irritating to an Instructor Who Irritates You

Don't cut class, drop the course, or transfer to another class when you have an instructor you find irritating. Instead, attend class and do things such as these that communicate your negative opinion.

Take a paperback book to class and read it while the instructor lectures.

If you knit, take your knitting to class and work on it instead of taking notes. Click the needles loudly if you can.

Sit back with your arms crossed and refuse to take any notes while everyone else is writing furiously. Scowl and sneer at those who are taking notes.

Use class time to clip your fingernails.

Just as the instructor leads up to an important point in the lecture, lean over and whisper loudly to a classmate. Include muffled laughs and snickers. Keep it up, pretending not to notice how distracting your whispering is to the class and how angry the teacher is getting.

USEFUL ALTERNATIVE: Be responsible for your feelings. When you blame others for your feelings you are letting other people control you. Consider what is happening as information about yourself and try to learn a lesson.

Talk Down to Instructors You Think Are "Losers"

If you have several instructors, you will probably feel that one of them is excellent, most of the others are adequate, and that one is a "not so great." Here is a good opportunity to sneer at, be sarcastic with, and show open contempt for a teacher. You can prove to other students that you are so tough that you can put down instructors to their faces.

USEFUL ALTERNATIVE: If you can't avoid being sarcastic, then consider not saying anything at all. It is tough enough being an instructor, especially when you know that some of the students openly dislike you. Instructors have all the fears that you might have if you had to make useful presentations to the same group day after day.

Remember, too, that it is a function of your human nature to like one of your instructors the best and another the least. If you really wanted better teaching, you could give the instructor a sincere compliment after a better-than-average lecture. You could do the various things we recommend at the beginning of this chapter to encourage good teaching. If you are critical of teachers in a way that is not helpful or useful to them, you need to have a target for your disgust more than you need good teaching; so don't take yourself too seriously!

Ask Your Instructors to be Personal Counselors

It's natural for you to want to be friendly with your instructors, but unfortunately, some students expect too much of them. These students expect their instructors to be terribly interested in all their personal ideas, interests, and problems. Most instructors want to be friendly with their students but are not in a position to be all things to all students.

The difficulties begin to arise when students begin dropping in all the time to talk, unload about their personal problems, and generally cut into the rather tight schedules within which many professors work. Professors often feel uncomfortable discouraging such calls. Few professors want to be known as uncaring or uninterested in their students. Professors want the best for their students and are usually willing to try to help. It's simply unfair to ask professors to spend their time socializing on the job or solving your personal problems.

USEFUL ALTERNATIVE: Try not to ask your instructors to do more than they are professionally equipped to handle. If you need help with personal problems, see the professional counselors at your college or talk to your best friends.

Demand that Your Instructors Give You Special Favors and Consideration

We've known students who will miss half of the semester and then ask if they can somehow get the information from the instructor. We've known students who would ask instructors if they could take the midterm two weeks late because they were leaving early on spring break for a vacation in Florida. Our favorite is the student who called an instructor at 8:00 a.m. on Saturday to find out if he missed anything important during the week of classes he was absent while vacationing in South America.

USEFUL ALTERNATIVE: Most of your instructors will be people who are interested in your academic and personal well-being. Instructors understand that you may run into financial, transportation, health, and numerous problems that interfere with successful performance in class. Don't be afraid to let your instructor know when an event drastically alters your performance. If you're ill with the flu for two weeks, let your instructor know why you're missing class. Instructors appreciate knowing why students aren't coming to class.

Minor problems should be kept to yourself. If your car breaks down and you miss class, don't come in with a big song and dance, expecting your instructor to pray for your car. Accept the bad with the good. Borrow notes from someone in the course. Don't expect your instructor to repeat an entire lecture for you.

In short, if something of tremendous importance necessitates asking a favor from your instructor, don't hold back! If minor irritations of life have made your student life a bit miserable, assume you'll recover. Don't throw your personal problems at your instructor. What you'll probably find is that you'll live happily ever after if you forget the past and proceed with the future.

HOW TO TURN A BAD SITUATION AROUND

Avoid Doing Poorly in Courses by Being Diplomatic and Willing to Work

If you are likely to receive a D or F in a course, you can often salvage a bad grade. But you have to learn to be diplomatic and pleasant to deal with. Too often, students having academic problems approach instructors with unbelievable stories, rather than accepting that a straightforward approach is best.

Talk to your instructor and ask for a chance to make up or improve your work. Go with a plan. Offer to make up or retake exams. Ask if you can write an extra paper or rewrite the project you threw together the night before it was due. Explain why you are willing to do extra work.

Instructors are much more likely to give students a chance to make amends if the students accept responsibility for their poor state of affairs. If you get caught in this situation you need to acknowledge responsibility for having done poorly. You need to acknowledge that you are willing to turn over a new leaf rather quickly. Most instructors will give you a chance. Bad grades are not permanent unless you allow them to be.

For example, if you do poorly on the midterm or final, for reasons other than you just didn't study, it is reasonable to ask to take a make-up exam. Ask for a chance to show that you do know the material. Maybe you didn't prepare correctly or you were ill. Things have changed now and it may be appropriate to ask for a chance to redeem yourself. Even if the instructor says you can't take the test to change your grade, ask to take it anyway to see for yourself if you can do better. Assuming that you get a better score, this will have a positive psychological effect on you and possibly the instructor.

If you anticipate a bad grade in a course because, for legitimate reasons, you haven't been able to turn in all the work, consider asking the instructor to submit an "incomplete" on the grade sheet. Your instructor may be willing to follow school policies that allow students to complete course work after the course is over. At most schools you have several weeks into the next semester to complete the work.

Reprinted by permission of UFS, Inc.

You can change the past if you want to. A sincere request for another chance, a specific plan about what you will do, and a commitment to do it may influence the sternest instructors and deans.

Whatever you do, don't just quit. If your college courses are overpowering you, you don't have to become a dropout. Don't just disappear or not show up for registration. Talk to your advisors and explore several possibilities.

Students are often unaware as to why they are facing difficulties. You may be in need of professional instruction in reading and study skills that is offered from academic support programs on campus. You may have personal problems getting in your way. Your college will have professional counselors to offer you guidance. Sometimes students just need a break from college, which in many colleges is called "stopping out." Your advisor may see a need for this and be able to arrange for you to take a leave of absence and come back later.

What is critical is that your colleges want you to succeed. But it will be up to you to seek help. The help is usually available if you seek it out.

SEEING INSTRUCTORS AS HUMAN BEINGS

The list of Behaviors Guaranteed to Frustrate Instructors is not meant to convey the message that instructors are special people who have to be treated with kid gloves. Absolutely not! Instructors are human beings who react to pressures, demands, problems, stresses, and all the other factors that complicate our lives.

Instructors are human beings just like you. They prefer to be treated nicely. They want you to come to their classes and learn every good thing you ever wanted to know. Most instructors will work overtime to help you. If you'll look for the good in your instructors and try to make their classes pleasant and enlightening, most of them will do everything humanly possible to make your life as a student as good.

But remember, if you ask too much of your instructors, cut into their personal lives, appear disinterested in their courses, or generally make a pest of yourself, you'll encourage them to be sullen and angry individuals. You'll hear instructors complain about not having enough time to get their work done. You'll hear professors gripe about students who don't show up to class, don't ask good questions, don't seem to be interested in learning, and are no joy to teach.

What we're suggesting to you is the simple fact that *you can make a difference!* You can choose to help your instructors be better instructors who enjoy teaching. In contrast, you can choose to behave in ways that cause instructors to be unhelpful and boring. Instructors who go around with a chip on their shoulders are often created by students who don't appear to care about their education. The choice is yours. We suspect you'll want to do your best to help your instructors do their best for you and your fellow students.

Accept the fact that you will have great instructors, mediocre instructors, and some who are less than desirable. Regardless, follow the suggestions we've made. Try to help every instructor be a good instructor.

❏ ACTION GUIDELINES: Turn Your Negative and Angry Feelings into Positive Actions

1. What behaviors or habits do you exhibit in a class that you don't particularly care for, which might result in your instructor developing a negative attitude toward you? List them below:

_____

_____

_____

2. What could you be doing instead to draw more positive reactions toward you? List the behaviors.

_____

_____

_____

3. Practice your new behaviors for a month. Then come back to this space and describe how your behavior has changed in the class. Discuss whether or not by behaving differently, you have developed a different attitude toward the class and the instructor.

_____

_____

_____

4. If your behavior in a class changed, did your perception of the class change? What does this tell you about the effects of your habits on your attitudes?

_____

_____

_____

SUCCESS GROUP ACTIVITY: Getting Better Teaching

With your friends and success group members decide which of the following strategies would be the best for all of you to try. Try not to take on too much. You want to figure out which would be best for you and focus on doing them well.

1.   Take some time with several classmates to develop a list of things which good teachers do. List specific, observable behaviors.

2.   Look at how your learning style might differ from the instructor's teaching style. Clarify what you might ask the instructor to do that would be useful for you.

3.   List all those things you might do that could be rewarding for an instructor.

4.   Observe each instructor to see how much or how little the desired teaching behaviors occur.

5.   List all the things that students do that can irritate, bother, and upset instructors and make teaching an unpleasant experience.

6.   Observe how you react when a teacher is less than what you would like. Ask yourself, "Do I do any of the things which upset and frustrate teachers?"

7.   Track positives. When an instructor is low in giving you good teaching behaviors, look for any little signs of improvement and immediately reinforce them.

8.   Compliment and reward instructors who do many of the things you list as good teaching. Be specific. Let instructors know what you appreciate. REMEMBER: The more quickly you reward a desired behavior, the more effective your reward.

9.   Ask yourself, "Am I a rewarding person to have in class?" If you aren't, then here is a good chance to practice. REMEMBER: Trite as it is, there is a lot of wisdom in the old idea of "An apple for the teacher!"

10.   Talk with each other about the results of your efforts. What went well? What did you learn? Compliment each other in the process.

SUCCESS GROUP ACTIVITY: Help a Teaching Assistant

Young teaching assistants (T.A.s) are often nervous. Many T.A.s have never taught before and are anxious to make the class go well.

With your group, decide on a few things all of you can do to help your instructor provide better instruction and feel more comfortable with your class. Choose a few things everyone in your group can do consistently. For example, if your T.A. appears to be interested in students' questions, make sure that you regularly have several questions about the readings or lectures.

If your T.A. lectures, members of the group should take good notes from which you develop questions. Show that you pay attention to the lectures by asking for just a few minutes to review the questions you have developed.

Naturally this procedure will work better with T.A.s who are interested in students' opinions. You may run into a T.A. who doesn't want to be bothered, who just wants to lecture and not be interrupted by students' comments or concerns. These T.A.s tend to be few and far between. Don't devote a lot of time to these instructors. Give your added attention to the T.A. who is really concerned and could use a little encouragement from students, especially well-prepared and interested students.

12

How to Develop Friendships and Gain Support From Your Family

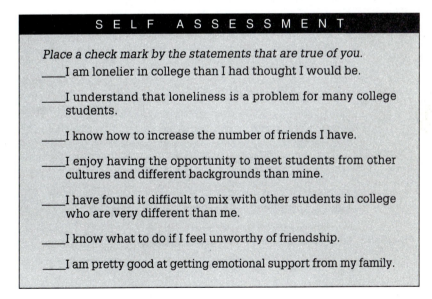

S E L F   A S S E S S M E N T

Place a check mark by the statements that are true of you.

____I am lonelier in college than I had thought I would be.

____I understand that loneliness is a problem for many college students.

____I know how to increase the number of friends I have.

____I enjoy having the opportunity to meet students from other cultures and different backgrounds than mine.

____I have found it difficult to mix with other students in college who are very different than me.

____I know what to do if I feel unworthy of friendship.

____I am pretty good at getting emotional support from my family.

Solving the Friendship Problem

Friendships are a great antidote against being vulnerable to the opinions and manipulations of strangers. Several good friends are also good for your enthusiasm for studying. It is hard to be enthusiastic about studying and learning when you feel homesick or lonely. Little energy is available for studying and learning when the need to be accepted and liked dominates your thoughts and concerns.

Fortunately, there are many things you can do to increase the number of friends you have and the amount of warm support you get from your family. It is not necessary to struggle through school with a rather lonely existence, hoping that things will get better later on.

Guidelines for Developing Friendships

As with success in school, you have choices about how many friends you have. Having friends is not a matter of luck or having money or having a great personality. Friendship develops between people as a result of a combination of variables that you can influence.

Have Frequent Contact

Research into the sources of feelings of friendship shows that the main contributing factor is *frequency of contact*. That is partly why we have emphasized so often in this book that a realistic plan for being more successful in school should include frequent opportunities to spend time with friends.

Research in college dorms, in housing projects, and in neighborhoods shows a consistent relationship between friendship and how often people have contact with each other. One study of married students in campus housing, for example, showed that couples living in certain apartments developed friendships more frequently than would be predicted by chance. These people were living in apartments at the foot of the stairs. Observation finally revealed that the couples were seen more frequently because the garbage cans were located near the bottom of the stairs!

Many such studies show that, in general, the closer you live to someone, the more likely it is that he or she will remain a close friend. Once you understand how frequency of contact influences friendship, you can see why certain conditions predict that some students will have fewer friends at school. Don't take a lack of friends personally if you are:

living at home instead of in student housing

not joining a fraternity or sorority

married to someone who is not a student

working full-time while going to school

studying all the time

training full-time for individual athletic events such as swimming or long-distance running

being a quiet loner who rarely talks to anyone.

To have more frequent contact with other students, get involved in one or more of the many extracurricular activities on campus. These include:

committees for student body activities, such as Homecoming or Parents' Weekend, or producing the yearbook

intramural sports

social-action groups such as Greenpeace or environmental causes

special-interest clubs and groups such as the psychology club, ski club, foreign students club, or photography club

school newspaper

church-sponsored social centers near campus.

A wide variety of activities is available to you that will bring you into contact with other students with similar interests. Keep in mind that it is not unusual for a beginning student to feel lonely. Loneliness is a normal experience when in a totally new situation without contact with old friends and family.

If you feel homesick, phone home. Write or exchange cassette tape letters with your family. Get a cassette tape recorder and make a short tape to send home. Your family would like to hear from you. Sending tapes from time to time will also help them make the transition with you as you assume your new role as an educated adult.

Obtain the addresses of several good friends from high school and write or send cassette tapes to them. Exchanging tapes will probably be better than writing because you gain much more from hearing a familiar person talking. Besides, people will often say things on tape about personal experiences that they wouldn't want to put into writing!

Be Assertive

Can you walk up to someone who looks interesting and initiate a conversation? If you are in the cafeteria can you go to a stranger, ask permission to join that person, and ask several questions that will help you get to know each other? Can you voluntarily offer your opinions or thoughts in a way that lets others get to know you?

Once you decide to take some initiative and to make a reasonable effort to create what you would like to have, you will find that your life works better. One of the important lessons of life is to learn how to develop friendships, how to be a good friend, and how to gain the support of other people. It could be that learning how to develop and maintain friendships and gain support will prove to be one of the most valuable abilities you learn in college.

NOTE: If you sit back passively and hope that others will go out of their way to be friends with you, you arc likely to be disappointed. Shyness does not have to be a terminal conditional unless you want it to be!

If you feel that you lack assertiveness, we recommend reading several books on becoming more assertive. They will provide excellent advice and examples on how to behave in ways that will help you improve your interaction skills.

Be a Good Listener

People like being listened to. They feel friendly toward a person who has a sincere interest in them.

How do you accomplish this? Ask questions and listen with an open mind.

Dale Carnegie, author of *How to Win Friends and Influence People*, states, "You can make more friends in two months by being interested in other people than you can in two years by trying to get other people interested in you." Why should other people be interested in you if you aren't interested in them?

So do not work at being liked. Work more at finding out what is likeable about each person you have contact with. Good listeners have a wide range of acceptance for what they learn about others. This is why so many people feel friendly toward a person who is accepting and tolerant.

A quick way to become more open-minded about other people and less judgmental is to develop the habit of mentally responding "That's okay" when you learn about another person's thoughts and attitudes.

NOTE: A judgmental person, even though remaining silent, eventually communicates through facial expressions, body language, and other reactions the attitude of "no one should think that" or "that's sick."

If the person you are listening to has attitudes and opinions that you dislike, the chances are poor that you will be a good friend of that person. You can have empathy for the individual, but you probably will not have much in the way of friendship.

Your behavior is contagious. Positive behavior creates positive reactions; negative behavior gets negative reactions.

If we compare observing, open-minded people with those who are more judgmental in their reactions, the ranges of acceptance and rejection form a continuum.

Open-minded and Judgmental Thinking Scales

Open-minded

accept	neutral	reject

Judgmental

accept	neutral	reject

Notice that the open-minded person has not only a wider range of acceptance but also a wider neutral range. This means that much of what is learned is neither accepted nor rejected. People respond well to this trait. On the other hand, if you constantly have a judgmental attitude about the way other people think and live their lives, frequency of contact with others will make very little difference and will not lead to close friendships.

Let People Know You

If you want people to accept you and like you, you have to let them know what you feel, think, and do. If people have very little sense of you as a person, there is little for them to relate to. Accept the fact that when some people learn about your feelings and thinking, they won't like what they hear. That's okay.

No matter what you are like as a person, someone is going to dislike you. That is the way the world works. Trying to avoid being disliked will prevent you from being liked. Allowing people to know more about you is the only way to gain the friendships and acceptance you need.

NOTE Putting on an act that impresses others creates a barrier to friendship. How? Because when people smile and show that they like you, a part of you knows it is your act they like. This makes their response emotionally dissatisfying. You tend to question how much you can really respect anyone who falls for an act such as yours. And you still end up feeling lonely because you have private thoughts and feelings that others don't see. Trying to come up with the perfect act is not the way to avoid feeling lonely. It is guaranteed to make you stay lonely behind a happy front.

Be Emotionally Honest

Did your parents raise you to be honest? Probably so. And did they raise you to hide certain feelings? Were you told, "Don't get angry, don't be selfish, don't complain, don't brag," and so forth? If so, you were raised to be an emotional liar. You were raised to deceive people into believing you do not have such feelings.

Your parents had good intentions, of course, because people who constantly express such feelings are very difficult to be around. The problem is that people who try never to feel angry, selfish, negative, or proud are also very difficult to be around. Expressing such feelings either too much or too little makes friendships difficult.

Feel Worthy of Friendship

If you do not feel worthy of friendship, none of the recommended actions will work for you. How do you react when people like you? Is it enjoyable or do you get embarrassed? When people tell you they like you, do you say "Thank you" or do you feel uncomfortable?

What is your opinion of people who like you? Is it positive or negative? Do you respect them or do you question their judgment? If you believe that anyone who likes you is a person of questionable judgment, you definitely have a problem!

If you feel uncomfortable when people make efforts to be friends with you, take a little time to make as long a list as you can in answer to these questions: What are all the good reasons people would enjoy being friends with me? In what ways am I a nice person to be around? What are all the things I like and appreciate about myself?

If you are uncomfortable about attempting to answer such questions, you may have been raised to avoid feelings of self-esteem. Conscious self-esteem is necessary, however, to function well in the world. As was discussed in Chapter 3, self-esteem allows you to accept people's praise and affections as legitimate.

Remember, it is not conceited to think well of yourself. Conceit means to feel superior to others and inform them about it. Self-esteem means to feel basically good about yourself even though you still have a lot to learn.

Visit the Counseling Center

Let's say that you have more frequent contact with others, listen well, are open-minded, express your feelings honestly, and yet are still shy and lack friends. There are books and cassette tapes at the counseling center on how to overcome your shyness.

You may want to have a few sessions with a counselor to talk about why you are so shy. It is possible that there is something from your home life that you have to be cautious about not revealing. Adult children of alcoholic parents are often guarded and try to present a "front" rather than being easily self-revealing. Go find out.

Friendships with Students from Other Cultures and Backgrounds

One of the most exciting things about going to college for many students is that they learn about cultures very different from the one they know. As a college student you have some rich opportunities for multi-cultural experiences. You have many chances to learn how to live and work successfully with people who may be different from you.

Which of the statements reflects your expectancies about how your college experience would prepare you to live and work with other people?

    ____ I expected the courses and instructors to expand my knowledge of the people who inhabit the world.

    ____ I looked forward to the opportunity to meet people who had very different religious philosophies than my own.

____ I hoped to meet and get to know people of all races.

____ I hoped to meeting people whose socio-economic status was very different than my own.

____ I looked forward to meeting people whose language and culture was different than my own.

____ I had hoped that by meeting and getting to know people different from myself, I would enhance my ability to work in positions that require good interpersonal skills.

The opportunities you have in college to meet and interact with people very different than yourself bring you many unexpected benefits. The observations of college graduates and their employers reveal many useful payoffs. Comments from students include the following:

"College helped me get rid of many of my stereotypes of what people who are different than me are like."

"Learning to work successfully with all types of people was as important as anything I learned in college."

"The world is changing so fast. It is getting smaller by the day. I really needed to learn to understand what people from other parts of the world were like and how they saw life."

"College really opened my eyes as to how little I knew. It is not that I have changed my values so much. What has happened is that I have a better understanding of why other people think and act as they do."

Comments from employers include:

"My company can't afford to hire people who can't listen to and appreciate another person's views. After all, we are selling to an international market. We must understand what people want and why they want it. Our sales people must know how to work with people who are very different from themselves."

"The number one thing our company looks for are intelligent people who can communicate. That means they can read, write, and learn effectively. Learning is a key. They must be able to get along with all types of people and

> learn from them. It isn't a matter of being a company person. What matters is that you are enthusiastic about meeting and working with all types of people."

> "No matter how you cut it, a person in our line of business has to be people oriented. You have to be able to get along with other people. That doesn't mean you can't have your own opinions. You have to appreciate the value of other people's ideas and be willing to learn from them."

The comments go on and on from directors of personnel, directors of training, office managers, owners of private businesses, and CEO's. Success in life requires that you appreciate the other person's perspective.

What is really rewarding is to talk with college freshmen who have stayed up until three in the morning in discussions with dormmates. You typically find that many freshmen say these discussions are more enlightening than some of their courses. That is what college is all about.

How to Gain Support from Your Family: Barbara's Story

It is easy to think, "If only my parents were different, things would be much nicer for me." That is true, of course, but not likely to lead to much improvement.

You have the ability, if you want to use it, to improve your relationships with your family. Once you develop the intention to change things, and start looking for ways to make small improvements, you can get some good results. Here is one example among many.

Barbara was starting her sophomore year in nursing school when she took introductory psychology. As a course assignment she was required to do a "behavior-change project." The project involved using principles of behavioral change with a person she had frequent contact with in daily life.

Other students in the class went to work on younger sisters, a neighbor's child, bus drivers, talkative roommates, boyfriends who drove too fast, smokers, overweight friends, and other available subjects. Barbara decided to use her father as the subject for her project.

Barbara lived at home and her relationship with her father was very poor. She said:

> We were always looking for ways to cut each other. He enjoyed saying rotten things about nurses to me. If he'd say "Good morning" to me, I'd say "What's good about it!" If I came home from school excited about something

and wanted to talk about it, he would just sit there in his chair and keep on reading. He didn't care about anything that was happening to me. Once when I was trying to talk to him about school, he got up and walked out of the room. Didn't say a word. Just walked out.

He is retired, so he is usually home during the day. I know he likes it if, when I'm home at lunch time, I make a bowl of soup for him. I'd go into the kitchen and make myself something. He would get his hopes up and then be disappointed when he saw I only fixed something for myself. Chocolate cake is his favorite, so when I baked something I made sure it was *not* chocolate cake.

When we were assigned the project, I decided to see if I could improve my life at home. It is hard enough getting through nursing school without always having a big hassle at home. I've been dreaming about going into nursing for a long time. It's exciting! I wanted my family to care!

Barbara's Plan for Herself

Barbara decided that each time her father responded pleasantly or positively she could be pleasant to him and do something special to show her appreciation for his interest in her. The slightest positive gesture from him would be immediately attended to by her. She would try never to overlook the slightest improvement, no matter how small or weak. Her goal was to increase the number of times her father showed interest in her and the depth of his interest.

Following the procedures recommended in class, Barbara outlined these steps:

Desired project goal: Father to greet me cheerfully each morning; show interest in what is happening at school; talk with me about school.

Current level of desired behavior: Seldom looks at me or listens when I am talking about school; never asks about school.

Reinforcements to father for increase in desired behavior: Bowl of soup at lunch, bake cookies and chocolate cake, smile and say "Thanks for talking with me," kiss on the cheek.

Three weeks later Barbara reported the results of her project to the class:

My first chance to use a reinforcement was during a lunch time. I talked with Dad for several minutes, and he listened without looking at his magazine. I didn't try to push my luck by going on too long, so I got up and asked him if he would like for me to fix him a bowl of soup. His face brightened up. He smiled and said "Yes."

In the morning if he said hello to me, I'd smile and say "hello" and kiss him on the cheek. Mornings are much more pleasant now.

After about three times fixing him soup at lunch, he began showing more interest and would ask questions. Then one evening he asked me to tell him about a book I read, and we spent almost 20 minutes talking. I immediately got up and went out to the kitchen and baked him a batch of cookies.

Last Friday afternoon I got home about 1:30. He got up from his chair as soon as he heard me come in and came over and said "I've been waiting for you. I would like to know more about what you are doing in school if you have time to talk." Did I ever! We spent *two hours* talking. That is the longest my father has had a conversation with me in my whole life! It was great! He was *really* interested. When we finished, I gave him a big hug, said how great it was talking with him, and went out and baked him a chocolate cake.

(Barbara suddenly grew quiet. Her eyes started to water, and she struggled to hold back tears. Her voice choked up a little as she went on.) Something happened this morning that isn't in my written report. I was getting ready to leave for school and Dad came up and put his arms around me. He said, "Barbara, I want to take you out to dinner next week. I want to get to know you better before it's too late."

Like many people who want their lives to be better, Barbara discovered that by changing how she interacted with her father, he changed in ways that she had hoped for. She took steps to improve how she and her father got along and he responded in positive ways.

When you are willing to try something different and are open to change old habits, you can change your life. Knowing how to modify your behavior on your own by learning directly from life's experience is an essential skill to develop because there will always be problems and challenges in your life that no one prepared you for and that no one can teach you how to handle well. You have to learn some things all by yourself—and that is the focus of the next chapter.

❏ ACTION GUIDELINES: Gaining More Support from Your Family

Most students want and appreciate support from their families. Yet students often report that they receive less praise and recognition for their academic accomplishments than they hoped for. In fact, it is not uncommon for a family member to be critical or to make discouraging remarks about academic pursuits.

If you have an upsetting conflict with a family member and would like to make things more pleasant, review Barbara's Plan for Herself. Then develop a plan of action that has a realistic chance of leading to an improvement.

To improve your contact with your family, however, you may also have to engage in some uncomfortable self-examination. Can you admit to yourself that you have been acting in ways that maintain the conflict?

If there are no big problems with your family members except lack of interest and support, develop a plan of action for yourself based on the principles described in this chapter. Think about how you would like things to be between yourself and your family, and then take the necessary steps.

❏ ACTION GUIDELINES: Developing More Friends

Review the chapter, outlining the principles related to creating friendships. Then select someone to test the principles on. Choose a person that you feel equal to, someone likely to have attitudes and interests similar to yours. To increase your chance of success, select a person who is easily available to you. Then you'll have more opportunities to have frequent contact.

Start by having frequent but brief contacts with the person. Develop the habit of saying "Hi!" as you walk by. Wave to the person as you pass. Nod and smile whenever you have an opportunity. Find out the person's name and say hello, using this person's name, every time you have a chance.

As you sense feelings of friendly recognition developing, be ready for an opportunity to ask the person one or two questions about himself or herself. Be specific. Ask, "How are your exams going this term?" or "What do you think of the president's announcement yesterday?"

Be willing to reveal your private attitudes or feelings briefly and then quickly focus attention back onto the other person. Don't be overly quick to like a person; don't be too eager, not at first.

Be a good listener. Listen with interest and an open mind. Try to learn what it is like to be the other person. Try to discover what is unique about this individual. Then, as you find out what he or she is really like, let yourself warm up more.

Don't be overly concerned if at first you feel that you are manipulating or doing what is so obvious that the person will see through it. People will be flattered that you are making the effort. What you're doing is acting as people do who have good friends. When you conduct yourself in a new way, at first you are very aware of it. But as you practice and see that it works, it gradually becomes a habit. You become unaware of what you're doing, and it becomes more natural for you.

❏ **ACTION GUIDELINES: A Friendly Challenge—Helping Someone Who Wants a New Start**

Do you feel concerned about someone who uses alcohol and other drugs too much? Would you be available to help that person if he or she wanted to stay sober and drug free? These are important questions to think about because students working with other students is the key ingredient to every successful rehabilitation program on college campuses.

At the University of Indiana significant improvements were made in large dormitories by creating friendship networks for students.

The STOP program (Student Opportunity Program) at the University of Massachusetts is a successful program for problem drinkers. It is proving more effective than individual therapy because it is based on holding sessions with groups of students instead of individual counseling. STOP has wide campus visibility and support.

The Palmer Drug Abuse Program requires all students to stop associating with friends who use alcohol and other drugs. It creates new friendship groups and shows students how to get all the emotional benefits and needs met that drugs did for them. Bob Meehan's approach is effective because it is realistic and practical. He has students talk first about what emotional needs they satisfy from taking drugs. Then he shows them how to satisfy those needs and more without drugs.

The key in every program, however, is new friendships and that is where you come in.

How about undertaking a worthwhile challenge? What if your success group, or you individually, offered friendship and some good times together to a fellow student wanting to get off drugs and alcohol?

If your campus has a program, how about volunteering to help out? If it doesn't, consider doing something on your own.

Our nation has a problem with drugs and alcohol. It is a problem in schools, on the highways, in the workplace, and in homes. But healthy, responsible lifestyles cannot be legislated. The solution to the problem of alcohol and other drugs is friends. Strong friends. Quality friends.

You can do something about the problem. You can make a difference.

❏ **ACTION GUIDELINES: Living and Associating with Substance Abusers**

Don't ask why they use the substance. A behavior that is explained or justified becomes more difficult to change. Don't listen to explanations.

Focus on feelings. Ask the person how he or she feels when high. Ask them how they feel when they don't use alcohol or other drugs. Use information covered in

Chapter 14 about positive and negative thinking. Discuss with the person the positives and the negatives of taking drugs. Then discuss the positives and negatives of not taking drugs.

Don't be judgmental. If you moralize, put them down, diminish them, or try to make them feel guilty, they'll go back to their old friends. Practice liking a person while disliking one of their behaviors.

Make a rule. You will *never* meet with them or go any place with them if they are high or on drugs. No exceptions.

Expect relapses. They occur. Don't take it personally.

Don't chase them down. Don't forgive them. If they miss a chance to get together with you, it is their loss. Don't feel responsible for their recovery. Bob Meehan says that 31 different efforts were made with him before the 32nd time succeeded.

Schedule sessions with them to cover these key areas in *Student Success*: self-esteem, effective study skills, how to develop friendships, and how to gain strength from adversity. Overcoming weakness and ineffectiveness in these areas will replace the need for substance abuse with better experiences.

Be sure to stay in good contact with your own support group. It would also be smart to let a counselor or someone with the drug and alcohol program know what you are doing just in case anything goes wrong. It is reassuring to know that if you get in over your head there is someone with professional training to call or see as a backup resource.

❏ **ACTION GUIDELINES: Develop Friendships with Students from Different Cultures**

Step 1—List the names of students different from you who you would like to know better while attending your college:

_____

_____

_____

Step 2—Describe the situations, places, and opportunities you will have to learn from them:

_____

_____

_____

Your learning may take place in classes, dormitories, fraternities and sororities, religious organizations, student groups and clubs, and from the many different types of social groups and organizations on your campus. Try to empathize with them. How would you feel trying to live in a place full of strangers who act, think, dress, and eat in ways different from what you have ever known?

SUCCESS GROUP ACTIVITIES

1.   Talk about what a good, solid, lasting friendship is like. Do you agree that being able to get angry at each other at times helps make the friendship better? How do you recognize a good friendship?

Discussions about good friendships identify the following as some important features. Look over the list and see what you agree with, what you would reword, and what you would add or change:

Friends feel equal to each other. Friendship cannot exist when you feel superior or inferior to someone.

Friends are comfortable being seen together, letting people know they are friends.

Friends reveal private thoughts and feelings to each other that they usually don't reveal to others. Their openness with each other is natural and spontaneous. They laugh together.

Friends can be trusted with confidential information. One of the fastest ways to destroy a friendship is to tell other people something you've been told in confidence.

Friends accept each other as they are. If you have a close friend, you allow that person to see you as you really are. You do not contrive or attempt to manipulate that person's perceptions of you to get that person to think of you in a certain way.

Friends see each other as unique. A friend says that no person on earth is quite like his or her close friend.

Friends have the freedom to disagree with each other. Friends can become irritated or angry if that's how they truly feel. You don't feel truly close to someone who is never angry at you. In any relationship the strong, positive feelings tend to disappear if negative ones are controlled and suppressed.

2.   Compare the inner, psychological factors affecting friendships with the information about Your Inner Resources in Chapter 3. Do you find similarities? Can you see how the ways you think and feel can affect both your success in school and your friendships?

3.   Discuss the process through which friendships develop. How do people become good friends?

Do you believe that good friends can get angry with each other and still remain friends? Discuss the steps described in Chapter 14 for handling anger between friends. How do the suggestions feel to you?

SUGGESTED READINGS

Bry, Adelaide. *Friendship: How to Have a Friend and Be a Friend.* New York: Grosset and Dunlap, 1979.

Emery, Stuart. *Actualizations: You Don't Have to Rehearse to Be Yourself.* Garden City, NY: Doubleday, Dolphin, 1978.

Glasser, William, M.D. *Positive Addiction.* New York: Harper and Row, 1976. This book has been around for a while and is available in paperback. It will give you some good insights into the desirability of healthy, "positive" addictions. Glasser describes how and why drug and alcohol addictions shrink a person's world and trap them in it while positive addictions expand a person's world and increase effectiveness. (Written before research into endorphins took place.)

Hearn, Janice. *Making Friends, Keeping Friends.* Garden City, NY: Doubleday, 1979.

Meehan, Bob, with Stephen Meyer. *Beyond the Yellow Brick Road.* Chicago: Contemporary Books, 1984. Read this book. It is highly informative. It will give you a good feeling for what you are dealing with from the point of view of a chronic drug addict who is very successful at rehabilitating young drug users. It will provide you with practical ways to be helpful.

Shedd, Charlie, ed. *You Are Somebody Special.* New York: McGraw-Hill, 1978.

Read the section on drugs in a recent introductory psychology textbook. Find out what all the various drugs are and how they affect the brain and nevous system. We recommend reading about drugs in James V. McConnell and Ron P. Phillipchalk, *Understanding Human Behavior,* Harcourt Brace Jovanovich, 1992.

part 5

How to Learn and Cope in the School of Life

- ❏ *Surviving Hazards and Dangers in College*

- ❏ *Anger and Negativism: Two Emotions That Can Defeat You*

- ❏ *How to Become One of Life's Best Survivors*

13

Surviving Hazards and Dangers in College

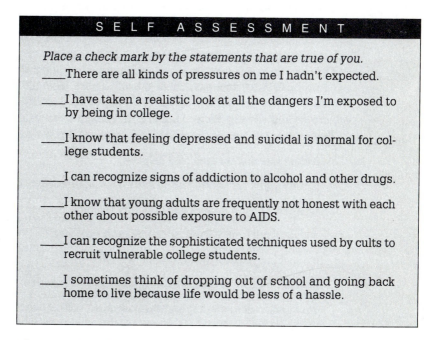

SELF ASSESSMENT

Place a check mark by the statements that are true of you.

____There are all kinds of pressures on me I hadn't expected.

____I have taken a realistic look at all the dangers I'm exposed to by being in college.

____I know that feeling depressed and suicidal is normal for college students.

____I can recognize signs of addiction to alcohol and other drugs.

____I know that young adults are frequently not honest with each other about possible exposure to AIDS.

____I can recognize the sophisticated techniques used by cults to recruit vulnerable college students.

____I sometimes think of dropping out of school and going back home to live because life would be less of a hassle.

The Hazards and Dangers

Going to college is a more dangerous survival test than many students realize. Stress, depression and suicide, abuse of alcohol and other drugs, exposure to AIDS, cult recruitment, and poor judgment can ruin your life and health or kill you.

To be successful in college and in life you must be alert to the many things that can do you in. Survival requires taking a look at the negative side of situations as a first step to taking preventive actions, and minimizing risks.

Things always happen, of course, that are out of our control. Christa McAuliffe had no way of knowing that a defect in the Challenger space shuttle would cost her her life. Each of us can, however, take action to reduce the predictable risks to our lives, health, and well-being.

Overwhelming Stress

It is normal to feel overwhelmed by college during the first few weeks. You left a familiar world with people you knew to enter an unfamiliar world filled with strangers. You changed status from being a successful senior in high school to becoming a naive freshman.

Life at college is complex, ambiguous, challenging, and fast paced. Protective adults do not save you from being irresponsible. You now make choices and decisions every day that affect your life.

Instructors load more work on you the first month of classes than you had to do in a year in high school. You may get lower grades than you are used to and feel inadequate for college. You may get homesick but going home is not a choice because your younger brother or sister has taken over your room.

The freedom to eat or not eat as you wish and to sleep or not sleep whenever you desire, can throw your physical health off balance. Your old friends aren't around. You may have broken up with your high school sweetheart, or worse yet, maybe you've been dumped because they found someone new.

Typical signs of feeling overwhelming stress and depression include:

feeling sad, discouraged, and helpless

feeling guilty for letting family and high school teachers down

sleeping 12 to 16 hours a day or hardly sleeping at all

withdrawing from friends, spending most time alone

not making yourself study, dropping grades

increased use of medications, drugs, alcohol

emotional outbursts—crying, anger, temper, self-criticism

over eating or losing appetite for food

feeling lonely, unhappy, unlovable, unlikable, unaccepted all the time

feeling that all chances for a good career are shot

considering suicide as the way to escape from the pain and distress.

NOTE: It is important to understand that unhappy feelings, loneliness, shyness, and awkwardness are all necessary for growth and development. These experiences are a *normal* part of your maturation and emotional growth. Young people who don't experience them remain immature.

Thousands of entering college students have these feelings. Most of them survive this difficult period, learn valuable lessons, and gain strength from their unhappy experiences. Some do not. Suicide is the second leading cause of death in teenagers. (Accidents, mostly automobile, are the leading cause.)

Stress research shows that people who are stress resistant

1. talk with family and friends about what they are going through. They do not withdraw from the people who care for them. They are receptive to love and support from people who care about them.

2. locate and use resources available. At college this means talking with the counselors in the counseling center, the health service, or at one of the church sponsored student centers.

3. accept that life has painful periods. They expect that somehow they will find a way to get through this. They tap into inner resources and problem solve the situation.

People in the Counseling Office Can Help

They won't have a miracle pill to get rid of unpleasant feelings; they'll have something much better. They will show you how to get through the unpleasant period while the natural emotional processes of self-healing are operating.

Self-referral is difficult for almost everyone, especially if you are afraid or concerned about giving people a bad impression. Try to remember, however, that it is *normal* to have "down" or lonely periods and that it is entirely okay to get assistance in overcoming them.

If your car gets stuck someplace with a dead battery, do you ask someone for a jump start? You'd have to do something. So when you are stuck in a deep "funk," get some assistance. Talk with the counselors. They know ways to handle situations that seem hopeless. You don't have to try to handle them by yourself. It is not a sign of strength to mask your feelings with drugs or put on a front of happiness. Emotional strength develops from feeling whatever you feel and letting another human being be close to you when things aren't working perfectly.

Alcohol and Other Drugs

A freshman wanting to be accepted and liked by other students is easily led into frequent bouts of drinking and drug use. According to Eugene Hakansen, director of a college counseling service, "The greatest instigator of alcohol and drug use in college is a friend. Roommates get roommates to try drugs, older students influence freshmen to drink and use drugs."

Bob Meehan, a recovered addict and alcoholic agrees. According to Meehan, founder of the Palmer Drug Abuse Program that has helped over 300,000 people, "Teenagers do drugs to gain acceptance." He says ,"Peer pressure to take drugs is so strong that one teenager in two will say he gets high before he actually does."

The National Institute on Drug Abuse conducted a nationwide research project looking into the use of alcohol and other drugs by high school and college students. The researchers found that the reason given most often for using any substance is "to have a good time with my friends."

Alcohol is used most frequently of all drugs. Approximately 80 percent of all college students report using alcohol in the last 30 days. About 5 percent drink daily. Over half of the male students and one-third of the female students engage in frequent bouts of heavy weekend drinking.

Approximately 20 percent of the students use marijuana in a thirty day period. About 7 percent use cocaine or crack.

Surveys show that very few students understand how addictive cocaine and alcohol can be. Following are some indicators that a person is addicted.

Signs of Substance Abuse and Addiction

Signs of addiction and substance abuse include:

using the substance more and more frequently

developing a toleration for it; needing a bigger dose to experience the effects, with the effect lasting a shorter time

feeling "off" when not using it; feeling shaky, anxious, edgy, or physical discomfort without it

having little awareness of how much used; believing usage is normal and under control

friends noticing personality changes, from happy, "up," social, and self-confident to unhappy, grumpy, withdrawn, depressed, fearful, and paranoid

friends, family, and acquaintances expressing concern, encouraging less use or stopping

person saying more than once "I could stop if I wanted to, I just don't want to"

rationalizing use, blaming other people, events, situations for use

becoming unmotivated, with performance at work or in school deterio-
rating—less done of poorer quality

having auto accidents, and an increase in traffic tickets (alcohol)

not remembering the next day what happened the night before (alcohol)

warnings from officials, notices of delinquent payments

trying to borrow money, making excuses for not repaying loans, selling
off belongings, maybe stealing money or items to sell

promising to improve when confronted, asking for another chance, asking to be trusted.

Most campuses have alcohol and drug counseling available. Keep in mind
also, that with some people alcoholism is hereditary. The evidence is strong
that a person with alcoholism has a different biochemistry than social
drinkers. Their bodies metabolize alcohol differently. It is a condition that
can be handled.

The Cults Want You

Lonely students are vulnerable to cults. Using sophisticated recruitment
techniques, cult members are skillful at offering warm, "unqualified positive
regard" to lonely students.

Cults feed on unsuspecting white, middle-class young people. Most vulnerable are students who were raised to be pleasant, cooperative, friendly,
trusting, and "good." Very few minorities or street smart kids from big cities
join cults.

A cult member who looks like a college student approaches a student who
seems sad, alone, and despondent. He or she greets the student warmly and
starts a conversation. After talking for a while, the student is invited to come
to an evening meal at someone's apartment with a group of friendly students.

The people present are extremely friendly, and interested in the new
guests. The student is given good food, warm smiles, personal interest, and
friendly touching. Before the student leaves, he or she is invited to come
along on a weekend retreat. It will be a chance to spend several days with
friendly, happy, college-age people who want something more from life than
just taking tests.

At the retreat the student is welcomed as a new member of a group totally
committed to making the world a better place. A leader that everyone respects
takes control. The student sits for hours without being able to eat, go to the
bathroom, or get a drink of water without permission. People stand up, one by
one, and share how wonderful their lives are now that they are enlightened and
free of their old games.

Group acceptance is conditional on being able to stand up and confess that you are guilty of playing manipulative games with people and are tired of living a life that is boring and unsatisfying. There is hope for you, however. This leader and group can help you break away from your old life. They will help you reprogram your attitudes, thoughts, and feelings to become like them.

What happens is a mental and emotional shift called "snapping." You suddenly feel joyous to be accepted by them. You understand why they had to trick you into the session. You return with instructions on how to identify and recruit new members. You may be so enraptured that you decide that your parents' way of life and a college education are trivial, empty, and meaningless compared to what you have now as your new life purpose.

Sex, AIDS, and Honesty

The first reports of AIDS released by the Centers for Disease Control showed that the highest risk came from intravenous drug use, mostly among people living in poverty. AIDS is spreading throughout the entire population, however. The likelihood of contracting it from heterosexual activity increased without much public awareness until the shocking disclosure in 1991 by professional basketball star Earvin "Magic" Johnson.

Of great concern is a research report on how honest sexually active young adults would be if asked by a potential sexual partner about recent sexual activities with others. About 40 percent of the men and 20 percent of the women said that they would downplay or deny sexual contact with others if asked by a potential partner.

Any sexually active young adult is at risk to contract some sort of sexually transmitted disease. Approximately 30 to 40 million adults in the United States are infected with genital herpes. About one million new cases of genital warts are reported each year. Four million new cases of chlamydia, 1.8 million cases of gonorrhea, and millions of cases of trichomonas are reported each year. In today's world good judgment and intelligent precautions are necessary to maintain one's life and good health.

Definitely Not Kind, Not Gentle

The openness of a college campus creates many opportunities for people who prey on others. You have to guard your credit cards against thieves who make charges or get cash advances against them.

It can be distressing to suspect that a dormmate may have stolen money or personal items from you. Or you could come back from a trip and discover that your computer and stereo have been stolen. Students with automobiles have their car windows smashed in by thieves looking for cassette tapes, car stereos, athletic gear, and other items.

On some campuses female students need to walk in groups or be escorted at night because of attacks by rapists. Women must also be cautious about going out on a date with someone new because of the risk of date rape.

You learn about students who cheat on exams or purchase a term paper and brag about it. You hear about intolerable things that instructors, administrators, and coaches sometimes do or say to students.

You hear that someone is saying horrible things about you to others. A student that you've just met may dislike you and make cutting remarks.

Not a Happy Camper!

The question is, what do you do when you must deal with a side of life that you wished did not exist? When the world that exists does not match up with your dreams and hopes? When, as your mom may have said, "You are not a happy camper?"

In the action guidelines that follow and the next two chapters we will provide some guidelines about how to gain strength from life's toughest challenges, how to increase your resistance to stress, become invulnerable to peer pressure to get into alcohol and other drugs, be untouchable by cults, and alert to potential dangers while remaining happy, trusting, friendly, and optimistic.

❏ ACTION GUIDELINES: Maintaining a Positive Attitude in Stressful Situations

I. Clarify what is negative and stressful to you.
    A. Make a list of everything you experience as negative or stressful.
    B. Discharge your feelings, if necessary: cry, yell, get mad, write in a journal, tell a friend; clear the system.
    C. Go through the list, item by item, asking questions:
        1. Could I do something about this? How direct is my contact?
        2. What if I ignored this or avoided contact?
        3. Could I change the situation in some way? Who could coach or help me?
        4. What if I changed my reaction to it?
        5. Why is this good for me? What can I learn from this?
        6. Next time what will I say or do?

II. Make a list of what is positive and revitalizing in your life.
    A. Review and reflect on pleasant experiences.
    B. Ask questions about how to repeat, increase, or have new positive experiences.
        1. Am I ignoring or taking for granted some positive aspects of my life?
        2. What do I enjoy doing? What do I get enthusiastic about?
        3. What would I like to do that I keep putting off?
        4. Who do I enjoy sharing good experiences with?

III. Take steps to decrease your exposure to negative experiences and increase your positive, revitalizing experiences. Give yourself permission to take some selfish actions.

SUCCESS GROUP ACTIVITIES

1. Have any of you known a student who talked about or attempted suicide? What are your feelings about that happening? What would you do if you felt so badly that you contemplated suicide? What would you want your friends to do?

2. What are the worst feelings you've ever felt? What are your worst feelings as a student? How do you manage to get through emotionally difficult times?

3. What are some of your concerns about AIDS? What facts do you have available? Have you ever associated with a person with AIDS? What are your concerns about sexually transmitted diseases? What precautions, if any, do you think a person should take?

4. Do you know anyone who has had to deal with date rape? Is this a subject that is discussed?

5. Have you ever been approached by cult members? Have you known of a person who became involved in one?

6. What are your attitudes toward alcohol and drugs? Do you know anyone who shows signs of being addicted? Can you confirm from your own experience the role that friends play in the use of alcohol and drugs?

14

Anger and Negativism—Two Emotions That Can Defeat You

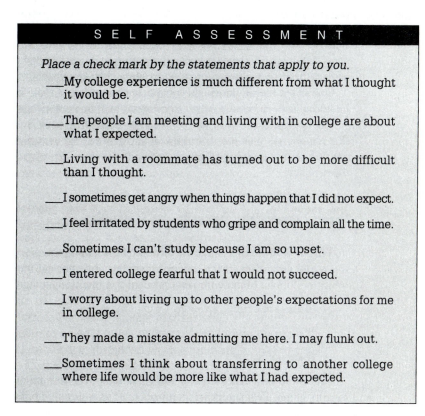

S E L F   A S S E S S M E N T

Place a check mark by the statements that apply to you.

___My college experience is much different from what I thought it would be.

___The people I am meeting and living with in college are about what I expected.

___Living with a roommate has turned out to be more difficult than I thought.

___I sometimes get angry when things happen that I did not expect.

___I feel irritated by students who gripe and complain all the time.

___Sometimes I can't study because I am so upset.

___I entered college fearful that I would not succeed.

___I worry about living up to other people's expectations for me in college.

___They made a mistake admitting me here. I may flunk out.

___Sometimes I think about transferring to another college where life would be more like what I had expected.

IS COLLEGE LIFE NOT WHAT YOU EXPECTED?

Most students find college to be very different than what they expected. This makes some students very happy; college life is better than they predicted. Other students are happy sometimes, but unsettled at other times. College is very different from what they expected.

Another surprisingly large group of students feels unhappy much of the time. College isn't what they expected in ways they don't like. Classes are not interesting. They couldn't get the classes they wanted. Their living situation is uncomfortable. They aren't adjusting socially. Friends are hard to make. The food is not what they expected. They have to work too hard. All in all, things aren't too hot.

Two Emotional Reactions

It is in our human nature to react to upsetting events with angry attacks or helpless complaining, the emotional equivalents of the "fight or flight" response to danger. Learning how to handle anger and negativism is essential because these emotional states can be very distracting when you are trying to study and learn. If you ever spent an evening in the library and accomplished nothing because you were too upset to study, you know what we mean.

One of the major, unofficial courses in college life is thus "Emotions 101: Learning How to Handle Anger and Negativism in Yourself and Others."

Our approach, as we've said before, is to emphasize that it isn't the situation that counts, it is your reaction to it that determines your success in college. So the first step to learning effective coping methods is to observe and describe the problem.

Unmet Expectations, Demands, and Frustration

Why is it so many college students express unhappiness, frustration, distress, and very often "pure" anger? There are a number of reasons, most of which boil down to these frequently heard comments of students:

"Things at college just aren't what I expected."

"People are placing too many demands on me!"

"I am not happy!"

When you hear comments similar to those above, they are often accompanied by anger. Few students recognize anger as a chronic problem. Most students think of anger happening only when they are subjected to other people's ill conceived acts, stupidity, and general carelessness.

From our perspective, the most useful description of the origin of anger and how you can learn to deal with it comes from an unpublished book manuscript on "The Anger Habit," by Professor Donald E.P. Smith, now retired from the University of Michigan and one of the world's foremost authorities on college reading and learning skills. Smith and his colleagues wrote one of the first great texts on reading and learning skills in the 1950s, *Learning to Learn*.

Different Forms of Anger

Smith's research demonstrated that college students have learned to react with anger to many different situations and express their anger in many different forms. Unless a person is overt, loud, antagonistic, or generally difficult to deal with we don't classify their behavior as anger.

Which of following would you interpret as ways of expressing anger?

crying

swearing

telling jokes about others

throwing and smashing things

leaving your room messy

going around feeling depressed

hiting a piece of equipment that doesn't work

feeling sad and lonely

not saying "hello" to someone who says "hello" to you

leaving a friend out of activities

throwing trash on the street

yelling at other drivers when you are driving

leaving a bathroom dirty

not pushing in your chair at the library

eating by yourself in the dining room

making nasty comments about your roommate

not going to class

failing to read your assignments

using drugs

not paying attention in class

acting snobbish toward certain people

Students express anger in many different ways. All of the items listed above can be ways of expressing anger. Anger can be expressed in ways so indirect the person is not conscious of feeling angry. This is because many children are made to feel guilty about feeling or acting angry. Instead of becoming a person who never expresses anger, however, their anger seeps out indirectly.

It is important to recognize that anger is normal and healthy. It is also important to understand that if you don't learn to handle your own anger well, you will not handle other people very well when they are angry. Their lack of control will overwhelm your shaky controls.

To understand the situation better, let's look at how anger can be triggered.

Unmet Expectations Are a Cause of Anger

Anger is usually the result of things not occurring as you expected. When you feel angry, you are reacting to something that wasn't what you had predicted.

Examine your expectations of college. How are instructors and courses different from what you thought? If you live in a dorm or apartment, how is living with a roommate different than you expected?

Here are some examples of what students report about situations with their roommates that made them angry. Do you identify with any of these experiences?

"I like having my roommate gone while I study but she's so popular I have to take over a dozen phone calls each evening!"

"My roommate is a slob!"

"When I was trying to study for an exam my roommate had his friends in to watch TV and eat pizza until after midnight. I was fuming."

"My roommate borrowed my car without asking permission."

"My roommate and her friends ate my food. When I told her I didn't like that, she said in her home the rule was 'finders eaters.' "

"I came back early on the weekend and found a stranger in my bed sleeping on my sheets. My roommate had told a friend of a friend it was OK."

In all of these instances something happened that the student had not expected and did not like. What do you do about these and other incidents? One is to take time to realign your expectations so that your expectations will be more accurate. The other is to learn how to express your anger in healthy ways and learn how to resolve the conflict.

How to Get Angry and Resolve Conflicts

You learn to deal with anger by learning to make more accurate predictions about what you can expect from other people and objects. Your best friend may arrive late to pick you up to go to a concert. You are late to class and your car won't start. In either case, anger won't solve the problem.

Keep in mind that it is not bad to feel angry. Your anger can help you learn what to expect next time. You can regard anger as "feedback." Feedback is information that tells you how accurate your thoughts and behavior were in a situation. Your anger often says to you, "Dang! I hadn't expected that. I have got to change things!"

Before we cover what to do, however, take a moment to think about ways of expressing anger that makes things worse and ruins friendships. Have you ever done any of the following? Has someone acted this way with you?

Unproductive Ways to Express Anger

Catch the person by surprise just as they are going out the door on a date or starting to fall asleep.

Blame them for your feelings. "You really upset me . . ."

Accuse them of bad motives. "You're trying to make me fail my courses."

Turn them into a no-good noun. (a nerd, a paranoid, a pervert, a sleeze bag, and so on)

Decide they are so bad and defective there is no hope for improvement. Decide "I will never again go any place with them."

Refuse to talk face to face. Refuse to reveal your feelings if they ask what is wrong.

Tell others how bad the person is. Gossip destructively.

If you want to express your anger in productive ways, improve the situation, and maintain a good relationship with the person, the following steps will be useful to follow.

How to Express Anger Productively and Improve the Situation

Ask for time to talk about something that is upsetting you. Warn them that you feel angry. Let them say when they are ready. (They will listen much better this way.)

State your feeling first, then describe the behavior that triggered it. "I feel angry because I saw you on campus wearing my best sweater."

("You . . ." statements are often hurtful, make the person defensive, and can lead to a permanent loss of friendship. "I feel . . ." lets you express your feelings and gives you a chance to work things out.)

Ask questions. Ask about why they did what they did. Ask if they are aware of the effect of their actions on you. "Don't you know that my aunt bought me that sweater in Italy and I only wear it at special times?"

Ask for what you want. "Please never again wear my clothing without my permission."

Discuss possible solutions. "I want you to agree that in the future you will ask first."

Thank the person for listening.

Does the idea of expressing anger directly to someone you like make you nervous? Have you heard the term "co-dependent"? Co-dependency is a term developed for partners of people with alcohol and drug dependencies. The co-dependent partner always forgives—even physical abuse—and makes excuses for their abusive partner.

In other words, "turning the other cheek" when you feel upset and abused can be a fine quality, but if practiced as a rule instead of an option, it can get you treated like a punching bag or a doormat. Part of being an emotionally strong person is being able to speak up to express angry feelings when you are bothered by what another person has done.

What to Do When Someone is Angry at You

Unproductive Ways to React to an Angry Person

Think back to how you have reacted when someone is angry at you. What have you learned from experience is a useful way to react if you want to improve the situation? Here is what people say does *not* work:

Get angry, argue back. "You're not easy to live with either!"

Interrupt the angry person to give them your explanation. (Anyone can create excuses and rationalize what they do.)

Refuse to listen. (It is not a sign of strength to refuse to listen.)

Use negative body language. Cross your arms, clench your jaw, look out the window.

Tell them not to feel angry. (First the person is angry and now you are telling them to not feel what they are feeling.)

Feel frightened or overwhelmed.

Believe that when they say they are angry at your behavior they are saying you are a bad person.

Tell them they're wrong.

Say "Yes, but . . ." What this really menas, said psychiatrist Eric Berne, is "I've let you talk for awhile, but now I'm going to explain how my view of this is the correct one."

If you want to frustrate people and have them go around telling others what a royal pain you are, then do the things listed above. If, on the other hand, you want to handle conflict in a way that leads to a good outcome and keeps your relationship healthy, then follow the steps listed below.

The most important thing to accomplish with an angry person is to *give them the experience of being well heard.* An angry person calms down fairly quickly when you have empathy for them and make a sincere effort to understand what you might have done to upset them. Here are the steps to follow.

How to Listen Well and Improve the Situation: Empathy Skills

Ask for it. Say "What is wrong?" "What are you angry about?"

Listen. Listen with the intent of being able to repeat back what they say.

Ask clarifying questions. "Have you been upset about this before?"

Listen.

Repeat back. The one time an angry person will be quiet is to see if you have heard them accurately.

Validate feelings. "I can see why you are so upset. I would be too." Learn how to validate feelings even if you don't agree with the facts.

If they're right, then apologize. "You're right, I should have left a note on your desk saying your father wanted you to call home right away. Just because I thought I'd see you in the library is not a good excuse."

Thank them for telling you face-to-face about their feelings. If you aren't a good listener they are going to tell ten other students about you. Better in your face than around campus.

Find out what they want. "What is your request if something like this happens again?"

Talk about how to handle similar situations in the future.

These steps are not guaranteed to work every time, but they increase your chances of having things work out well and help you maintain control when others lose control. Keep in mind that repeating back what people say to you is a powerful way to let them know you heard them. This is how to show empathy when it really counts.

The main challenge, however, is learning what triggers your angry feelings. According to Smith, "the feeling of anger is automatic and a necessary part of learning. But the rest of the anger experience, all the ways in which we express it, all the damage we do with it, to others and to ourselves, all of these follow-up events result from learning."

One of the thorny problems with learning to have angry reactions to unexpected events and then not express your feelings is that when you suppress (or "stuff") your feelings you become a candidate for cardiac problems, ulcers, and migraine headaches.

We've covered how to handle your feelings in healthy ways when they occur, but let's go back to the matter of what triggers the anger reaction in the the first place.

A Learned Habit Can Be Unlearned

Feeling angry is natural, but you don't need to get into the habit of continually feeling angry whenever your expectations are unmet. You can learn to deal with unmet expectations in better ways. You can reduce the amount of time you go around acting in angry ways.

As you learn to expect things, like the car starting when you turn the key or a friend greeting you pleasantly when you say "hello," you can learn to deal with unpredicted events.

Let's say you've been invited out by someone you are very attracted to. You hope this relationship can blossom into something greater than a mere friendship. You anticipate a pleasant romantic evening alone with your date.

Your date arrives. He or she comes to the door and you see that there is a car parked outside with another couple. The show and dinner you thought the two of you would enjoy alone will now include another couple.

Do you act disappointed? Cold to the other couple? Miffed that you didn't know more of the particulars of the date. Do you place demands on your date? Do you tell him or her that in the future you would prefer knowing if the date includes more than the two of you? Do you tell him or her that you do not want to go to this particular restaurant or show?

Why do we ask these questions? Because the way that most of us deal with our unmet expectations is to get angry and place demands on other people. We expected certain things. They didn't occur as we had predicted. Now we get angry and start demanding things. We are determined to control someone or something so that our predictions can be met, if not now, in future situations.

Is there a reasonable alternative in the dating situation we described to being angry and placing demands on others? You might say to yourself "I didn't think they'd be coming along. Next time I'd like to know exactly what's happening. I'll make the best of tonight. The next date can possibly be more to my liking." If you can find a way to have a nice time you may discover that these are your date's best friends and you are the person they've been looking forward to meeting.

Unlearning the Anger Habit

Everyone picks up habits from living with their parents. In some families the parents' way of getting cooperation was to make threatening demands "You'll eat what I give you or I'll really get mad at you." The child may learn that making angry demands is the way to get people to act differently.

Sometimes the child learns that the only way to get attention is to have temper tantrums. In some families an alcoholic or abusive parent is the only role model for the child. Whatever the origins, reacting with anger is a habit that is learned. It is also a habit that can be unlearned.

Do you recognize the "Anger Habit" as common to you? Do you often get angry when things don't go as you expected? Do you often respond to your unmet expectations with excessive anger? Do you see yourself as a person who when things don't go his or her way, starts placing a lot of demands on other people? If so, welcome to the club. There is nothing the matter with you. You are just another person who can learn why people act angry and that there is a better approach to dealing with unmet expectations than anger.

Dumping the Habit

You can learn a different way of reacting when your expectations are not met. How would you feel and how would you respond to people who said or did the following things to you?

Situation 1   You are late to pick up a date. When you arrive, she or he says to you, "Just why can't you get here on time? I feel embarrassed standing out here in the lobby. People think I am being stood up!"

Situation 2   Your roommate says, "Why do you always keep the room such a mess? I keep telling people what a slob you are. Would you please try to keep this place more orderly? After all, I live here too! I am really embarrassed when people come into the room!"

Situation 3   You are late to class. The instructor looks at you coming in the door and says, "I would really appreciate you arriving on time. It is very disconcerting to start a lecture and have people interrupt!"

As you answered the previous questions, you might have thought to yourself, "The person had a right to be miffed, although they could have been more diplomatic." The mistake they made was acting angry. People are late and people are sloppy. But trying to control them by placing demands on them just results in more anger. Many people feel "attacked" when we place demands on them.

The anger occurs when what people predict doesn't occur. The result of the anger is the demand or attack. This habit of getting angry when our expectations are unmet and then attacking other people or ourselves leads to much unhappiness. There is a reasonable alternative. That alternative requires that you look at yourself and ask the following questions:

How can I learn to accept that anger is not a problem?

How can I learn to accept that my unmet expectations may lead to anger, that anger is part of the learning process?

How can I learn to respond to the anger that develops by not placing demands on other people or attacking them?

What are reasonable responses when my expectations are unmet?

What expectations do I have about college that may be unreasonable?

How have I responded to my unreasonable expectations?

Have I placed a lot of demands on other people? Do I spend a lot of time attacking other people?

How should I respond rather than placing demands or attacking?

How can I learn to gather the information I need so that I can establish realistic expectations about the people I live with?

How can I gather the information I need to develop realistic expectations about what I can expect from my courses and professors at college?

A Solution

Being angry and trying to control people through anger and demands is common to most people. Once you learn to recognize when you have unrealistic expectations, you can learn to create expectations which reduce your anger. You will also learn to recognize that periodic anger is a normal behavior. Your anger tells you to change your thought and behavior processes. You needn't respond to people with anger or place demands on them. You know there are better ways to deal with situations and people who don't act as you had predicted.

Often, after we are angry and act in ways which make us feel uncomfortable, we say to ourselves "I didn't like acting that way. Why did I act that way?" Now you know. You have unrealistic expectations which are unmet and you get angry. It is no big deal. You simply want to learn to recognize your anger and act in more appropriate ways.

The alternative to being a person who is dominated by the anger habit is to collect information, to learn about the world as it really is, and to develop problem solving strategies that allow you to deal with the unexpected and what you want to change.

Negative feelings are not "bad" either. They happen. They are normal. They are part of a healthy emotional life.

At the end of Chapter 13 we outlined a plan of action for avoiding feeling chronically unhappy, helpless, and hopeless. It showed how to have a learning and coping reaction to the stresses and upsetting events at college instead of practicing a victim reaction when something upsets you.

That is what *Student Success* is all about. We want to help you learn ways to develop successful relationships with people and make learning at college a happy experience.

❏   ACTION GUIDELINES: How to Handle Yourself with Negative People

One of the most difficult challenges when you want to be positive about your life, however, is having to associate with negative, whining, complaining people. The key to effective coping is to understand that their constant complaining is not the problem. *The problem is that you have a negative attitude about their negative attitude!*

If you really want to be less distressed by all the negative talk that is typical of many college students, try these responses:

Tell them, "You may be right." Then be quiet. Just let their negative talk drift out into space. Don't try to change them.

Withdraw attention. Be impolite. Their complaining is an adult form of crying. It gets them attention. Withdraw your attention until they say something positive.

Listen and then say, "It is much worse than you know." Tell them about some major problems they've never mentioned. Beat them in their own territory and then go have a pizza with a friend.

Ask them to stop. Be very direct. Say, "I can't handle that right now." They may surprise you.

Say, "What you are talking about is not useful to me."

Tell them your mind is your territory. Ask them to stop broadcasting their complaints into your territory.

Ask them what they want. Ask what their plan is for handling the situation.

Don't tell them what is positive. Ask if they can see something positive. If you specialize in the positive view all they have left is the negative side. Learn how to give them room for another perspective.

❏ ACTION GUIDELINES: Managing Your Anger

Step 1. Write out a brief description of a recent situation that made you angry.

_____

_____

_____

Step 2. What expectations did you have which were unmet? Were your expectations realistic? How did you show your anger?

_____

_____

_____

Step 3. What would have been a more reasonable response?

_____

_____

_____

SUCCESS GROUP ACTIVITIES

1.   List some of your original expectations about college which may have proven to be unrealistic. Did you feel anger to having your expectations not met? How will you go about changing your expectations?

In the future, when you recognize anger developing due to unmet expectations, how might you go about preventing yourself from placing demands on other people and acting in unproductive, angry ways?

2.   Talk about the problems that develop when a roommate comes from a family in which it is OK to borrow dad's car, wear a brother's good shirt, or take $20 from mom's purse without permission. What can roommates do when habits that were the norm at home are intrusive, upsetting, and a violation of another person's space?

3.   Read what psychologist Martin Seligman has written about "Learned Optimism." Discuss your reactions to information that a person can replace pessimism about future life events by learning to be optimistic. Is learning an optimistic attitude something that appeals to you? Do you think a pessimistic person would be optimistic about succeeding at learning optimism?

15

How to Become One of Life's Best Survivors

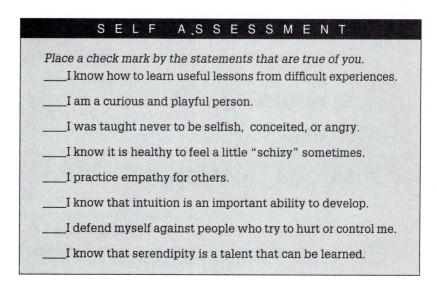

SELF ASSESSMENT

Place a check mark by the statements that are true of you.

_____I know how to learn useful lessons from difficult experiences.

_____I am a curious and playful person.

_____I was taught never to be selfish, conceited, or angry.

_____I know it is healthy to feel a little "schizy" sometimes.

_____I practice empathy for others.

_____I know that intuition is an important ability to develop.

_____I defend myself against people who try to hurt or control me.

_____I know that serendipity is a talent that can be learned.

Experience Really Is the Best Teacher

College is a *structured* learning environment. The school of life is an *unstructured* learning environment. Your ability to learn important lessons from life's experiences will mean the difference between how poorly or how well you live your life.

When you find yourself in a bad situation, do you let yourself become a victim or do you find some way to cope with it and learn valuable lessons? You don't learn to be "street wise" in college. Life's best survivors learn directly from experience.

Students with divorced parents, a mentally ill parent, or an alcoholic parent often have more emotional strength and good coping skills than students from stable, trouble-free homes. Children who have to cope early with a stressful, unstable adult world are often made stronger by the experience (Wolin, 1992).

Learning What No One Can Teach: How to Develop a Survivor Personality

People who handle life best have a knack for turning difficulties into growth experiences. They keep positive attitudes in negative situations. This is why viewing life as a school is practical and useful. When trouble develops, you gain strength every time you struggle to learn how to cope with something up-setting or difficult.

For example, in the chapter on working with instructors, we suggested using difficulties with your instructor as a way to learn to handle people better. Throughout the book, our approach has been to show you how to handle the difficulty in a way that makes you a stronger, more capable person.

Students who frequently use alcohol and other drugs remain at the same emotional level. Their nervous systems miss important learning experiences.

Self-Managed Learning

There is an old saying, "Good mariners are not created by calm seas." In fact, the purposes of the Outward Bound program are based on the observa-tion that when ships sink at sea, the old-timers are more likely to survive the hardship than younger, stronger people.

During the Depression in the 1930s, a few people went against the tide and refused to be swept away by mass despair. Even though thousands were des-titute, some people found ways to be happy and to enjoy being alive. Using their imaginations and inner resources, they maintained a positive direction for themselves and their families during hard times.

Learning from parents, teachers, and others is important, but adults who are life's best survivors have retained from childhood the self-motivated, self-managed ability to learn directly from experience. They process their experiences in a way that lets them treat everyday life like a school.

Throughout *Student Success* you have found at the end of each chapter activities designed to help you stay in touch with learning on your own. The sequence for learning lessons in the school of life goes like this:

1. Look forward to a new experience as a chance to test yourself or gain useful knowledge.

2. After any experience, whether planned for or not, reflect on it. Replay the whole thing in your mind. Relive the feelings, actions, body language, and words as it all happened.

3. Describe the experience. Write it down, tell a friend, or talk to yourself about what happened.

4. Evaluate your actions. How well did you do? What would you do differently if you could do it all over again?

5. What can you learn from the experience? About yourself? About specific people? About human behavior?

6. The next time you are in a similar situation, what will you do? Imagine yourself doing what it would take to get the outcome you desire.

For the person who is a constant learner, life is a never-ending school. Everyday experiences offer many rich and valuable lessons. One of the main purposes of a good education is to teach you good learning habits and how to manage your own continuing development. Your best teachers show you how to go beyond their teaching.

The real excitement in learning comes when you move past the level where others can tell you what you should learn or know. People who explore, grow, and develop are people who take risks. Self-managed learning develops your self-confidence. Self-esteem is necessary because what works best for you is not always approved by others, especially when you confuse them by being unpredictable.

Be Flexible and Adaptable

Life's best survivors are flexible and adaptable. They have many ways of reacting to situations.

Before reading further about the survivor personality, take a moment to look at the following list and check any traits that you possess. Add any not listed in the blank spaces at the end.

___ tough	___ sensitive	___ messy	___ neat
___ gentle	___ strong	___ cooperative	___ rebellious
___ independent	___ dependent	___ lazy	___ hard-working
___ shy	___ bold	___ consistent	___ unpredictable
___ proud	___ humble	___ playful	___ serious
___ selfish	___ unselfish	___ pessimistic	___ optimistic
___ logical	___ creative	___ _____	___ _____

If your reaction to this short self-assessment was something like "I'm all of these!" you are in very good shape. People with survivor personalities are paradoxical. They can be both one way and the opposite. They are serious and playful, selfish and unselfish, logical and creative.

Do you recognize this pattern? You have seen it many places in this book. In Chapter 1, we described how *Student Success* is built on the principle that you can both be a good student and enjoy your college years to the fullest. You also read that students most likely to reach their goals are both optimistic and pessimistic about what lies ahead. Later, in the chapter on learning and teaching styles, we emphasized the value of being both "external" and "internal," both right-brained and left-brained, in adapting to various instructors.

People who can be only one way—such as serious but not playful—are greatly restricted in what they can do. Being one way but not the other is like having a car with no reverse gear. Paradoxical or counterbalanced pairs of personality traits make you flexible and give you control over what you do.

Many children are raised to never be selfish, unhappy, negative, conceited, dishonest, and so on. Unfortunately, people who try to go through life acting like good five-year-olds are emotionally handicapped. They don't learn and grow. They try to put on an act with people. They have very little mental or emotional flexibility.

Develop Psychological Fitness

Psychological fitness, flexibility, and strength are derived from a solid base of successfully counterbalanced psychological traits. Physical fitness and strength derive from having flexor and extensor muscle groups in counterbalanced, controlled opposition. Similarly, our emotional flexibility, and to some extent our digestive fitness and energy, are derived from having our sympathetic and parasympathetic nervous systems in counterbalanced opposition.

It fits nature's pattern to regard psychological fitness as derived from a complex mix of opposite psychological traits. Some students are relieved to learn that being both one way and the opposite is not a symptom of being "schizy." They are reassured to know that being both friendly and unsocial, for example, is a sign of psychological strength. The key is to feel good about being paradoxical instead of being upset by it.

Signs of high level psychological fitness include: flexible stability, relaxed intensity, pessimistic optimism, selfish unselfishness, self-critical self-appreciation, loving anger, moral lustfulness, cooperative non-conformity, and responsible rebellion. In other words, life's best survivors seem to be successfully schizy!

The checklist was not intended to be complete. It was intended to make the point that the more pairs of paradoxical traits you acquire, the more complex you are and thus the more successful you can be in dealing with any situation that develops.

Be Playful and Curious

Being complex is not enough, however. In any difficult situation, it is essential to quickly assess and understand what is occurring. The capacity to quickly read, assess, and respond to situations develops as a result of a lifetime of playful curiosity.

Have you ever been to a high school commencement where a graduating senior was honored for being the best student in the class at asking questions? Not likely. But people best at handling life's survival challenges ask good questions and are good at "reading" people and situations. Questions are a sign of an absorbent mind.

Life's best survivors orient themselves with questions. They have questioning brains. They habitually ask questions such as:

How did they do that?

Why didn't this work?

Why did I do that?

I wonder why people do such things?

What would happen if . . . ?

What if I did the opposite from what people expect me to do?

How could I find out about . . . ?

This sort of curiosity gives a person experience in handling unexpected developments, unknown circumstances, and bewildering situations. Survivors are drawn to the unusual, the complicated, and the mysterious. Thus, when a difficulty develops, your habit of being open to the new and unfamiliar predisposes you to find out quickly what is happening. Then, by being playful, you have much better control over the situation than you would have if you just felt helpless.

Develop Good Defenses

To be a survivor requires you to defend yourself well. High self-confidence, strong self-appreciation, and a self-determined sense of what is right or wrong for you makes it possible to shrug off hurting, unhelpful criticism. There will always be people who have negative things to say about you. There will always be people who try to "con" you, threaten you, show that you are wrong, manipulate you, and "seduce" you. Survival requires being able to handle all these instances and to move past them. In this respect survivors are similar to the healthy person described by Maslow:

> Sales resistance, advertising resistance, propaganda resistance, opinions of other people resistance, maintenance of autonomy, suggestion resistance, imitation resistance, prestige resistance, are all high in healthy people and low in average people.

Be Synergistic

Life's best survivors have a strong need to get things working right. In reference to the Maslow hierarchy of needs, the need to have things working well is described as a need for synergy and would be placed above self-actualization.

One consequence of this need for synergy is that people with survivor personalities are very good to have around. They have a knack for doing the little things that count. When some difficulty develops, they are "foul-weather friends." They show up to see what they can do to help out.

They have a paradoxical selfishness and unselfishness in their way of life. When faced with conflicts and problems they ask themselves, "How can I interact with this so that things turn out well for all of us?"

Do you know someone like that? If you had an important group project to work on, is there a person you hope would be willing to participate? If so, what is it about that person that makes him or her so valuable to work with?

Be Open-Minded and Creative

The ability to survive situations depends on being able to read them accurately. Reading situations accurately results from having an open mind. Life's best survivors learn about the world without condemning it. They expect human beings to be human. They expect each human being to be unique and to have an individual perspective. They absorb information about what exists just for the sake of knowing.

A person with a closed mind quickly condemns or finds something wrong at the first impression. As shown on page 176, he or she quickly views things as right or wrong, and quickly thinks of people as being good or bad. The closed-minded person avoids empathy, and isolates herself or himself from accurate information about what is happening.

When you were a child, if your parents asked what you had been doing, and if you told them the truth, would they punish you or react in some very negative way? Most children learn that there are some things parents can't handle, and so children withhold information from parents about what they are really doing, thinking, or feeling.

Regardless of how unpleasant the information is, there is not much to be gained from becoming disillusioned. To view life as a school means that you can see human faults without becoming cynical. You discover that some students cheat during tests. You discover that the instructor doesn't catch the cheating or ignores it.

Research shows that people who score highest on creativity tests are people who are open-minded. Closed-minded people score the lowest on tests of creativity. To be creative is to come up with unusual ideas that work.

By understanding the relationship between open-mindedness and creativity, the survivor pattern becomes more clear. People with the survivor personality are very complex. You're never quite sure what they are going to do in any situation. Yet because they read the situations quickly and accurately and have the intention of having things work out well, their solutions are often creative and successful.

Follow Hunches, Use Intuition

Creative people are aware of subtle inner feelings. Sometimes survivors sense that something is wrong without knowing what it is. A tight stomach or an uneasy feeling can alert them. These feelings can be set off by anything—a person's tone of voice, something not said, a group's quietness, anything at all that doesn't fit.

Most people have more capacity for hunches and intuition than they realize. All of us have nervous systems that process information subliminally. The problem is that many people don't scan their bodies for signs of subliminal perception. (See any introductory psychology textbook for more about this topic.)

The ability to read and respond to subtle inner feelings gives survivors an ability to follow hunches. In general, women are better at this than men. Women are known to be intuitive because women are usually raised with emotions as an important part of their lives. Men in corporate life, more than women, need training on how to be intuitive.

Use Both Reason and Feeling

Survival often results from allowing oneself to be guided by feelings. A survivor's actions are not controlled by only emotions or logic. Survivors are influenced by both. There is a harmonious interaction between mind and emotions. With survivors, when emotions are likely to become disruptive, the objective mind can take over and maintain control. When you are more relaxed, survival may result from scanning your emotions for clues about what is right or wrong.

As we mentioned earlier, each of us has two brains. Survivors can use both the right brain and the left brain well. They can engage in nonverbal, emotional, musical, visual, intuitive, irrational, and metaphorical thinking. They can engage in logical and objective thinking. They are not limited to only one way of thinking or the other.

Develop Empathy for Others

The people who survive best in a variety of situations have empathy for others. They can quickly "read" the emotional states, attitudes, and perceptions of others. Experts in any field are usually high in empathy skills. They can step outside of their own feelings and perceptions to take into account the feelings and perceptions of others, even when disliked.

The empathy of survivors is not that of a weak, easily hurt "bleeding heart." It is more like the empathy of a defense attorney who must accurately understand the case against his or her client in order to prepare a good defense. Their empathy includes having an understanding of people who live and think in unpopular ways.

The attitude present in the empathy described here is "whether I enjoy you or dislike you, I am going to understand you as well as you understand yourself—and maybe even better." With this kind of empathy some survivors are in such good control that they can joke and play with their attackers.

It Isn't the Event, It's Your Reaction to It

People with survivor personalities rarely stay upset about what has been lost. They do not remain distressed when things have gone badly. They focus on the future. They know that nothing can be done now about what has happened. They accept responsibility for turning things around. They accept reality as it is. They accept responsibility for their reactions to conditions.

Martha Washington once said:

> I am still determined to be cheerful and to be happy in
> whatever situation I may be—for I have also learned
> from experience that the greater part of our happiness or
> misery depends upon our dispositions and not upon our
> circumstances.

Humor Makes a Difference

The ability to laugh and joke during a crisis is very practical. Laughing has a direct effect on one's ability to solve problems efficiently and deal with situations. Examples from television and the movies are Kate and Allie, Bill Cosby, and Michael J. Fox in the roles he plays.

Why does humor help? Laughing reduces tension. Creative problem solving, accurate thinking, and physical coordination are best in moderate emotional states. In athletics, the coach of a football team wants the linemen worked up to a high emotional state. In sports such as basketball, tennis, or baseball, a more moderate level of emotional arousal leads to better performance.

The humor used by survivors is directed toward the immediate situation. It is aimed at playing with the situation and poking fun at it. It is as though the person has the attitude, "I am bigger than this situation. This is my toy. I am going to play with it."

The person seems to be asking, "How does this look from a different point of view? What would happen if I turned it upside down? What if the reverse were true? What unusual things exist here?" By playing with the situation and toying with it, the person keeps from being overwhelmed and at the same time is likely to come up with a way to survive.

The Serendipity Talent

As you facilitate your own inner growth, you become increasingly competent, humorous, resilient, durable, playful, and free in your life. You spend less time struggling to survive than others, you survive major adversity better, and you enjoy life more.

When people with survivor personalities talk about difficulties they've been through, they are likely to say, "I hated going through it, but it was the best thing that happened to me." Such a statement shows that the person learned so much from the experience that it truly was beneficial. Life's best survivors react to life as a school and learn some valuable lessons about themselves and others. They are able to convert misfortune into good luck.

Terry Anderson was held as a hostage in Lebanon for almost seven years. He was subjected to many hardships. At the press conference after his release he was asked how he felt about having so many years of his life wasted. He said "They weren't wasted years," and talked about many positive things about his experience. His sister, sitting next to him, said, "He is different. He is better."

Some stories are dramatic, others less so. One never knows what an ordinary incident might lead to.

How Would You React?

Imagine renting a rustic wooden cabin in a beautiful forest setting for your honeymoon. The place is delightful. At dawn, however, a woodpecker starts its loud, rat-a-tat pounding on the roof. The noise is so loud you can't sleep. It happens at dawn the second morning, again on the third morning, and so forth.

What would you do?

Many people say they'd shoot the bird. Some say, "Who cares? It's your honeymoon."

This incident is a true story about a young cartoon illustrator and his bride. Their names are Gracie and Walter Lantz. By the time they returned from their honeymoon they had created the cartoon character "Woody the Woodpecker." He was the illustrator, she was the voice.

Decades later, when interviewed in their home on their fiftieth wedding anniversary Gracie said, "It was the best thing that ever happened to us."

The term serendipity was created by the English author Horace Walpole many years ago from the title of a story he heard as a boy. The story was about three princes who lived in the land of Serendip. Their father, the king, had them educated by the best teachers in the land. He knew, however, that they had not been tested by life itself. He pretended to get very angry at them and banished them from the kingdom to survive on their own. The story of "The Perigrinations of the Three Princes from the Land of Serendip" is an account of how the princes managed again and again to convert accidents and misfortune into good luck.

Walpole didn't remember the story entirely accurately but he was correct in observing a special human capacity to turn an accident of unexpected difficulty into a good outcome through the use of wisdom. Serendipity is not merely a lucky coincidence or discovery. Personal wisdom and effort must contribute to the good outcome.

❑ ACTION GUIDELINES: Developing a Talent for Serendipity

You can learn how to gain strength from adversity by discovering within you a talent for serendipity. To turn unpleasant difficulties into valuable learning experiences and convert misfortune into good luck, ask yourself serendipity questions such as:

How can I interact with this so that things turn out well for all of us?

Why is it good for me that this happened?

What can I learn from this?

How might I turn this around and have everything turn out well?

What would be useful for me to do right now?

Is there an opportunity here that I never expected to have?

The next time something like this happens what will I do?

What is amusing about this?

Questions such as these are the best way to organize your energies toward having things turn out well. By developing a talent for serendipity, you learn that when you are hit by adversity or misfortune you have a choice. You can dwell on your version of "If only other people would change, my life would be much better," or you can make things better for yourself.

Because you are a human being, you have an inborn capacity to learn what no one can teach you. To develop this talent, select a problem you are trying to handle right now. Ask the serendipity questions and take your time looking for answers. Write your questions in a diary if you like and talk with yourself about what answers you discover. By doing this, you may learn how to convert a major difficulty into the best thing that ever happened to you!

❏   ACTION GUIDELINES: Review Your Self-Assessments

Review how much you've learned about how to succeed in college in such a short time. Look back through the Self-Assessment lists at the beginning of each chapter. Check off the items you left blank the first time.

Appreciate yourself for how much you have learned in such a short time!

SUCCESS GROUP ACTIVITIES

1.   Now that you've had some weeks together, what do you think about a person's need for acceptance in a friendly group? Discuss whether or not having a friendly support group has helped you. Could you have done as well in your learning efforts without your support group?

2.   Talk with several classmates who are happy, stable, capable, and seem to be good survivors. Find out what their lives have been like. Ask them to talk about several of the worst experiences they've ever gone through. Try to find someone who was physically abused, had an alcoholic parent, or grew up in an unusually hard situation. Find out how these classmates learned to cope. Do they say they benefited from what they went through?

3.   In your experience, have parents and teachers facilitated or interfered with survivor personality traits?

Have you ever heard of a graduation ceremony in which a student was honored as being the best in the graduating class at asking good questions?

Were your parents supportive of your negative or angry feelings sometimes? Of your feeling proud of yourself? Of your making selfish requests at times? Have you heard parents or teachers tell a child to be only one way and not the other? To always by unselfish, for example, and never selfish?

Did you ever hear of parents or teachers being comfortable at hearing a child talk about precognitive dreams or mind reading?

Is it reassuring to know that it is desirable to be both one way and the opposite?

4.   Can you relate to the idea that experience is the best teacher? What does it mean to you to be told that a survivor personality can be learned but can't be taught? Can you see value in working at both getting a good education and learning important lessons from experiences outside the content of the course?

5.   Compliment each other on what you've seen each other accomplish! Have each person take a turn receiving compliments and appreciation from each of the others in your group. Is a celebration of your successes in order? Do something to reward yourselves. You deserve praise and appreciation for what you've accomplished.

A Concluding Observation

You are living in a world much different from what your parents and teachers grew up in. To survive and thrive you must find ways to orient yourself quickly to new circumstances.

You will probably have three or four careers during your life. National boundaries are blurring. To succeed in your career or professional calling you must be able to adapt to people from different cultures.

Critical thinking skills will be essential for handling rapid changes, conflicting perspectives, changing values, and unexpected developments that carry both opportunities and dangers.

In this book we have done more than provide practical ways to handle the challenges of surviving and succeeding in college. We talked about how, in every challenging situation, your reactions and strategy for interacting with something new and difficult is usually what determines the outcome.

In other words, we hope that the guidelines for surviving and succeeding in college help serve as a model for ways to cope well throughout your life. We wish you well!

Appendix

How to Make Athletic Goals and Academic Goals a Winning Combination

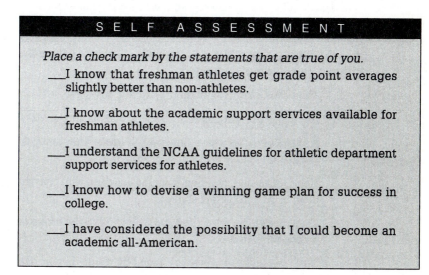

SELF ASSESSMENT

Place a check mark by the statements that are true of you.

___I know that freshman athletes get grade point averages slightly better than non-athletes.

___I know about the academic support services available for freshman athletes.

___I understand the NCAA guidelines for athletic department support services for athletes.

___I know how to devise a winning game plan for success in college.

___I have considered the possibility that I could become an academic all-American.

Academic All-Americans

Some of the best athletes in football, basketball, baseball, soccer, track, volleyball, swimming, and other sports are able to compete while also doing very well academically. At a national level many of these athletes are recognized as "academic all-Americans."

It is true that a few colleges with highly competitive sports programs let a few marginal student athletes slip by to keep them eligible to play. The average athlete, however, does as well in college as his or her classmates.

A study of the academic effects of freshman participation in varsity athletics, conducted by the Educational Testing Service and the American College Testing Program, shows that "on measures of persistence and grade-point averages, the athletes did as well or better than a matched group of non-athletes at the end of the freshman year. This finding held true across the 57 participating institutions, despite their diversity in size, selectivity, and athletic prowess."

This report, *Athletics and Academics in the Freshman Year: A Study of the Academic Effects of Freshman Participation in Varsity Athletics,* was developed for the American Association of Collegiate Registrars and Admissions Officers and the American Council on Education. The report was prepared with the assistance of the College Board.

A most revealing finding is that athletes who were predicted to have a grade point below 2.0 in their freshman year did better than non-athletes who had similar preparation for college. The athletes' grades "were higher than predicted—and higher than the grades of the non-athletes against whom they were matched. In fact, relatively few athletes earned grade point averages that were much below a 2.0 regardless of their SAT or ACT test scores or their high school grades."

Why do student athletes do so well, considering the extra demands on them? There are many reasons:

They work closely with their academic advisors.

More than other students, they use academic support services.

Athletes know they have little time to waste. They apply themselves well in the limited time they have for studying.

They get special attention from the coaches, who constantly encourage them in their academic studies.

Their motivation to succeed and their ability to be persistent at hard challenges help them.

They respond to failure and defeat by trying harder. Many bright students give up too easily when they encounter failure.

Academic Support Services

Do you know what support services you need? If so, do you know how to get the help you need? Research has shown that students who use academic support services are more likely to succeed in college. Use the following checklist to indicate what resources you need.

I could benefit from:

___ advice and help from an academic advisor who understands my special needs

___ improved reading and study skills

___ better writing skills

___ tutorial assistance with difficult courses

___ having a personal mentor to talk with

Academic Advisors

Does your athletic department offer the services of an academic advisor? If so, seek advice. Consult him or her regularly regarding the courses you are interested in taking.

Academic advisors to athletic departments usually have unique backgrounds that equip them to deal with your academic and personal problems. They have talked to hundreds of student athletes. They know which courses will best suit your interests and skills. They can also help you with special scheduling arrangements. Did you know, for example, that you might be able to take some classes in the evening with continuing education students?

Reading Improvement and Study Skills

Does your athletic department provide financial support for courses in reading improvement and study skills? If so, sign up right away.

By using the information and skills in *Student Success* and taking a course that encourages you to practice these skills, you will get the best possible start in your career as a student athlete.

A course in reading improvement and study skills will serve the same function as your athletic practice sessions. The course will encourage you to try new techniques that will make an immediate difference in your reading speed, comprehension, and efficiency as a student.

NCAA guidelines will allow athletic departments to financially support reading and study skills courses. If your athletic department hasn't started this type of program, ask your coach or academic advisor to investigate the possibility.

If a course is available but your athletic department can't supply the financial support, consider investing your own funds. Most reading and learning skills centers offer inexpensive courses. You may even find that the courses are free.

Writing Improvement

If you didn't know already, your college admissions tests showed you how good your writing skills are. Good writing skills are very important in college. They are closely related to college success. If you know that you aren't very good on written assignments, papers, or answers on essay tests, make improvement in this area a high priority.

Most colleges require freshman composition courses. Many of the instructors who teach these courses will not have a tremendous amount of time to give you individualized instruction.

It will be to your advantage to seek additional assistance from someone who can assess your strengths and weaknesses and spend the time necessary to improve your writing skills.

Check with your academic advisor to determine if individualized writing instruction is available from the athletic department, a campus tutorial program, or the English department.

If you can't find a writing instructor, make arrangements with a friend to critique one another's papers. A close friend will often tell you things about your writing that other people will not. This is no time to be sensitive. Get all the help you can.

Tutorial Assistance

A tutor is an especially skilled person who is available to work with you privately. Does your athletic department offer tutorial assistance? If so, try to find tutors who are either upper-level undergraduates or graduate students. Ask other members of your team for recommendations of outstanding tutors.

You want tutors who know how to teach you how to study for courses rather than tutors who simply want to reteach the course content. By picking up the study skills and tricks of the trade used by successful students, you may decrease your need for future tutorial assistance.

Mentors

Does your athletic department have a mentor program? Mentor programs are established to help students adjust to the demands of a university.

A mentor program is one in which a faculty or staff member at your college will volunteer to be your personal link to the university community. Your mentor will be available to talk with you about your personal concerns and introduce you to social and cultural aspects of university life that might otherwise escape you.

Mentors often act like those friends or relatives away from home who help you orient yourself to a new city. Once you are comfortable, you may see them less often, but you always know they are available for assistance.

We have found that mentors often become good personal friends with student athletes. They help you adjust to the demands of university life and at the same time show you a university often never seen by many students.

The Overall Game Plan

Your college may offer other support services than those we have mentioned. Making immediate use of support services may be your key to a successful college career. Receiving academic support is no different from receiving daily instruction from your coach.

Very few first-year student athletes can step into the starting lineup without at least a year of college coaching. Academically you are probably in a similar position. To crack the academic lineup, find out where you need help and get the best assistance offered. Often you will find that with a little help you can soon adjust to the academic demands that initially appeared to be insurmountable.

Eliminate Self-Defeating Actions

To be a winner you know that you have to avoid costly mistakes and errors. In sports the turnovers can kill you. Many contests are determined by the loser making too many mistakes, errors, fouls, or turnovers. That's why you spend part of your practice time working to eliminate self-defeating mistakes.

When you show up for the game or contest, you dress and act like a winner. You dress and act with confidence and enthusiasm. What would your impression be of a team that showed up late for a game, with many members in sweatsuits, and players slouched around on the benches not paying attention to the coach? What if during the game they shrugged off turnovers and missed chances to score. What would you think?

If this description amuses you, try running through your memories of student athletes in their classes. Do you recognize any of these self-defeating actions?

Do You Create Bad Impressions with Your Instructors?

Instructors sometimes have negative opinions and biases about students. Have you ever had to take a class from a teacher who had a bad impression of you? It's no fun. Once a teacher has a negative opinion about you and your work it is very difficult to change it.

Some student athletes, however, seem to go out of their way to create bad impressions. Too often we have seen students act in ways that cause instructors to believe that they are unmotivated, irresponsible, and inconsiderate. Some student athletes act like college would be great if only they didn't have to study and attend classes!

The negative first impression that some students trigger in classmates and instructors frequently results in a negative stereotype that is hard to overcome. For example, here are some ways that student athletes create negative impressions. If you are not a student athlete, ask yourself, "How typical are these behaviors of myself and my friends?" College instructors and professors were asked, "What biases do you have against student athletes and how did they develop?" They said:

> When students come to class wearing their athletic shirts and sweat clothes, they stand out from other students. If I were their coach, I would discourage athletic garb. It sets them up to be discriminated against by people who don't care for college athletics.

> Some athletes sit at the back of the room. Often they talk to one another during class. I assume they aren't interested in what I have to say. They just want to be as far away as possible and wait for the hour to be up.

> Athletes tend to sit together, seldom mix with other students, other than talking occasionally to attractive girls. They seem to be uncomfortable with other students. Maybe this is a sign that they don't feel they fit in. I would like to see them mix with other students.

> Athletes sit near the door with their jackets on. They don't appear to be taking notes. I wonder how they think they'll do well in the course.

> One fellow attends class about 50% of the time. He never tells me why he was absent. When he learns that he has an overdue assignment, he acts as though I am being unfair because he won't receive full credit.

> I set up an appointment with two players. They walked in 45 minutes late. I had another appointment in 15 minutes and couldn't do much for them. They acted as though it were no big deal, then asked if they could see me the next day.

> Some students who are athletes never ask questions. I wonder if they read the assignments.

One group of athletes, who I really like, unfortunately continually come in late. I try hard not to let this upset my routine. It is disturbing. I must have mentioned this to them three times. They don't seem to get the picture. They are fine once they are in class. I just wish they weren't late.

Several athletes frequently miss my Friday class at 1:00 p.m. I know they are often on the road on weekends. They must assume I know their schedule. They are polite enough to come in on Monday and mention they were on the road. Why not let me know beforehand?

Several of the football players let their beards go all week. On Friday they look like bums. I don't care what they look like. But the other students appear to be joking about them. I think this hurts their image.

A big lineman drags himself to my morning eight o'clock and falls asleep at least once a week. Having a 280-pounder sleeping in class is a bit of a distraction.

One jock turned in a paper the other day that looked as though it was scratched out on a note pad while he was watching television. The paper was wrinkled, dirty, and torn off a pad with jagged edges.

The bad impressions given by a small percentage of student athletes serve as an example of how any student can cause negative biases in instructors. Some working students who come into class late wearing dirty work clothes or students alienated for some reason do the same thing, however. The capacity to create bad impressions is available to everyone!

SUCCESS GROUP ACTIVITY: Creating and Reversing Bad Impressions

Are you willing to play with this situation a little? Try reversing your perspective. Answer this question: "If I purposefully wanted to cause instructors to develop negative opinions and biases against me, what would be my plan of action?" Write down your answers on a sheet of paper. Have fun thinking about the outrageous things you could do.

After you've developed your plan for self-destructive actions in the classroom, use it to increase your self-awareness. Ask yourself, "Do I ever do any of the things that would be part of a purposeful plan to create bad impressions with instructors?" Your answer to this question can tell you how to avoid or improve some bad impressions you may have created without knowing it.

Some athletes who read early drafts of this chapter and developed action guidelines to create more positive impressions reported these activities:

I would get to class early. As I walked in the door I tried to make eye contact. I wanted the instructor to be reminded that I was there early.

I tried to sit at the front of the class. I always take notes and try to keep eye contact with the instructor.

I never sit at the back of the room. I try to sit with people I don't know, so that I avoid talking with anyone during class.

If I arrive late for class, I always apologize to the instructor after class.

During discussion sessions, I try to raise questions over the readings. I make sure I am not always the first one to ask a question, but I find the teaching fellow always looks in my direction.

If I haven't had enough sleep, I always have a cup of coffee. I don't want to look sleepy in morning classes.

I made up questions from my notes. I made appointments with my discussion leader and asked him to look at my notes and questions to see whether I was looking at the important ideas. At first I felt funny doing this, but I found that the instructor appreciated my interest in his opinion.

Every paper I turn in I have somebody proof. I know my spelling and punctuation need improvement. Also, every paper is typed.

I try to make friends with one person in the class who isn't an athlete. When I have to miss class, I make arrangements to borrow that person's notes. I always let the instructor know when I am going to miss and that I have borrowed notes.

I have one instructor who always likes to talk to the students before class starts. I make it a point to get there early. He likes to talk about sports and he always wants to find out about the last game.

These statements from reports of action guidelines emphasize how to be realistic about what can work for or against you. We should add, however, that many students figure these things out for themselves. A senior who reviewed this chapter said:

One thing that I did my entire career was never to wear my letter jacket to class until I took several exams or turned in several assignments. Even though I had a 3.8 average I was wary of professors who might discriminate against me because I was an athlete. After the instructors found out I was a good student, I would wear my letter jacket to class. By that time I felt I was on safe ground.

Your actions affect your instructors' opinions of you as a student. In the following space, write five actions you can take that will show your instructors you are serious about learning as much as you can in their courses:

1. _____

_____

2. _____

_____

3. _____

_____

4. _____

_____

5. _____

_____

REFERENCES

Chapter 1

Smith, Laurence N., Ronald Lippitt, Lee Noel, and Dorian Sprandel. *Mobilizing the Campus for Retention.* Iowa City: ACT, 1981.

Adapted from Warren Willingham. *Success in College: The Role of Personal Qualities and Academic Ability.* New York: College Entrance Examination Board, 1985.

Bennett, Janet. "Transition Shock: Putting Culture Shock in Perspective" *International and Intercultural Communication Annual* 4 (December 1977): 45–51.

Chapter 4

Willingham, Warren W., *Success in College: The Role of Personal Qualities and Academic Ability.* New York: College Entrance Examination Board, 1985.

Chapter 7

Lindgren, Henry C. *The Psychology of College Success.* New York: Wiley, 1969.

Chapter 8

McKeachie, W. J., Donald Pollie, and Joseph Speisman. "Relieving Anxiety in Classroom Examinations." *Journal of Abnormal and Social Psychology* 50, (January 1955): 93–98.

Chapter 10

As used in this chapter, the term *myth* means "a collective opinion, belief, or ideal that is based on false premises or is the product of fallacious reasoning" (Funk and Wagnalls, *Encyclopedic College Dictionary*).

Chapter 11

Appleby, Drew C. *Journal of Staff Program and Organizational Development* 8, (Spring 1990): 41–46.

Chapter 13

Fondacaro, Mark R., Kenneth Heller, and Mary Jane Reilly. "Development of Friendship Networks as a Prevention Strategy in a University Megadorm," *Personnel and Guidance Journal.* 62 (May 1984): 520–523.

Chapter 14

Smith, Donald E.P., and Carl C. Semmelroth. *The Anger Habit.* Unpublished, 1987.
Seligman, Martin. *Learned Optimism.* New York: Knopf, 1991.

Chapter 15

Wolin, Steven, M.D. "How to Survive (Practically) Anything." *Psychology Today* 25 (Jan/Feb 1991):36–39.
Maslow, Abraham. *Motivation and Personality.* New York: Harper and Row, 1954.
Selye, Hans, M.D. *The Stresses of My Life,* 2nd ed. New York: Van Nostrand Reinhold, 1979.

ABOUT THE AUTHORS

Timothy L. Walter received his Ph. D. in educational psychology from the University of Michigan. He became Vice President for Student Development at the University of Tulsa in July 1992. From 1981 to 1992 he was a program director at the University of Michigan Reading and Learning Center and a faculty member in the Division of Kinesiology. Prior to returning to Michigan he held a tenured position in the Department of Psychology at Rhode Island College. During the past 25 years he has published widely in the areas of academic support, student retention, adult learning, childhood autism, and juvenile corrections. He is one of the pioneers in the freshman year experience movement. Tim and his wife Beverly have been blessed with Jeremy Holdsworth Walter and two wonderful twins, Sarah and Kathryn.

Al Siebert received his Ph.D. in clinical psychology from the University of Michigan. He is an adjunct professor with the Professional Development Center, School of Business, Portland State University. He is nationally recognized for his research about the personalities of life's best survivors. His findings have been published in books, newspapers, and national magazines. He has been interviewed about the survivor personality on *The NBC Today Show* and other television programs. For information about his book, *The Survivor Personality*, write to him at P.O. Box 535, Portland, OR 97207.

Tim Walter and Al Siebert are co-authors of *Learning Psychology*, a student manual to accompany *Understanding Human Behavior* by McConnell and Philpchalk.

Timothy Walter is co-author of *The Mountain is High Unless You Take the Elevator: Success Strategies for Adult Learners.*

Al Siebert is co-author of *Time For College: The Adult Student's Guide to Survival and Success.*

ACKNOWLEDGMENTS

There are many people to whom we owe much:

Beverly, Jeremy, Sarah, and Kathryn Walter, whose constant smiles and warmth make life such a pleasure.

James V. McConnell, our mentor and friend, whose passing will not diminish the example he set for us as a teacher, writer, and scholar.

Wilbert J. McKeachie, who created a stimulating environment at the University of Michigan for learning how to teach.

Donald E.P. Smith, John Hagen, Glenn Knudsvig, Dee Edington, Harry McLaughlin, and Joyce Linderman whose interest in and support of our work is greatly appreciated.

"Bo" Schembechler and Gary Moeller of the University of Michigan Athletic Department, whose support over the past eleven years has provided many opportunities to learn more about the world of student athletes.

Laurence Smith for his many excellent contributions to the Instructor's Manual for *Student Success*.

Eve Howard for her steady support and strong enthusiasm for "the book that every college student should read."

Our mothers, who were always proud of their sons.

Lewis H. Walter whose inspiration as a father and writer will never be forgotten.

FEEDBACK REQUEST

Please let us know how you did! How was *Student Success* helpful to you? How did having a success group work out?

Do you have any suggestions on how *Student Success* could be improved? Write to us c/o:

> Psychology Editor
> Harcourt Brace Jovanovich College Publishers
> 301 Commerce Street
> Fort Worth, TX 76102

Weekly Schedule

HOUR	Sunday	Monday	Tuesday	Wednesday	Thursday	Friday	Saturday
7–8							
8–9							
9–10							
10–11							
11–12							
12–1							
1–2							
2–3							
3–4							
4–5							
5–6							
6–7							
7–8							
8–9							
9–10							
10–11							
11–12							

Weekly Schedule

HOUR	Sunday	Monday	Tuesday	Wednesday	Thursday	Friday	Saturday
7–8							
8–9							
9–10							
10–11							
11–12							
12–1							
1–2							
2–3							
3–4							
4–5							
5–6							
6–7							
7–8							
8–9							
9–10							
10–11							
11–12							

Weekly Schedule

HOUR	Sunday	Monday	Tuesday	Wednesday	Thursday	Friday	Saturday
7–8							
8–9							
9–10							
10–11							
11–12							
12–1							
1–2							
2–3							
3–4							
4–5							
5–6							
6–7							
7–8							
8–9							
9–10							
10–11							
11–12							

Weekly Schedule

HOUR	Sunday	Monday	Tuesday	Wednesday	Thursday	Friday	Saturday
7–8							
8–9							
9–10							
10–11							
11–12							
12–1							
1–2							
2–3							
3–4							
4–5							
5–6							
6–7							
7–8							
8–9							
9–10							
10–11							
11–12							